Angels Sometimes Suffer

Angels Sometimes Suffer

The Lina Joy Story

Governor Joy and Bobby Alvarez

Writers Club Press
San Jose New York Lincoln Shanghai

Angels Sometimes Suffer
The Lina Joy Story

Writers Club Press
an imprint of iUniverse.com, Inc.

For information address:
iUniverse.com, Inc.
5220 S 16th, Ste. 200
Lincoln, NE 68512
www.iuniverse.com

ISBN: 0-595-18539-8

Printed in the United States of America

To the glory of God,
To all His angels,
To the miracles that walk among us every day,
and
To Santo.

Thank you for showing us that each
day we are given is a gift.

*Now to Him who is able to do exceedingly abundantly above all that we ask
or think, according to the power that works in us, to Him be glory in the
church by Christ Jesus to all generations, forever and ever. Amen.*
Ephesians 3:20-21

ACKNOWLEDGEMENTS

Thank you to all those who prayed for us.
I feel so blessed to have such a loving
family and wonderful friends. Words
simply cannot express my gratitude.

Governor Joy

CONTENTS

PREFACE

Yesterday, while rummaging through the last of the boxes from my wife's office, I unexpectedly came upon a single folder which contained probably the three most important papers to ever affect my life. The documents were not impressive-looking papers like my marriage certificate to the lovely Avelina (Lina, for short) Van Putten, or Dina's or Brian's birth certificates, or the Department of Defense Form 214 detailing my retirement after 20 years of naval service. Instead, the documents were innocuous-looking objects: a church bulletin, a welcome card, and a match letter.

The church bulletin, which actually started the entire chain of events described in this story, was from 1989. I was not in church with Lina that day; I had left months earlier on one of my many highly classified missions aboard an attack submarine. As I read over the bulletin, I finally saw what had grabbed Lina's attention: inside was a short, three-line American Red Cross announcement requesting that potential bone marrow donors come forward to help save a young man from our local high school.

While at work in the dentist's office the following week, Lina had apparently decided to have her blood tested; she did not, however, qualify as a match for the desperate student. Since she had already done the hard part by getting tested, the American Red Cross volunteers asked her to do something simple: assent to having her blood type information entered into the National Marrow Donor Program database to see if she might someday match someone else. The welcome card in Lina's box was a short form letter from the National Marrow Donor Program which simply said,

"Thank you very much for your charitable offer; we will call you when we find a match for your marrow."

The match letter, sent seven years after Lina's initial application, was from the American Red Cross Marrow Donor Program, and stated somewhat matter-of-factly that Lina had indeed overcome the rather astronomical odds to qualify as a donor for an anonymous recipient. Lina had come home ecstatic the day she received the match letter, sure that beating the odds was proof-positive that God had placed his stamp of approval upon this potential act of charity. I was at once awestruck at the mathematical improbabilities of such a match and impressed at the faith, love, and hope which defined my wife.

The reason I consider the bulletin, card, and letter so important? Because, unlike the thousands of bone marrow "harvests" which go off without a hitch, my wife's harvest went terribly wrong, resulting in a tragic series of ever-worsening infections, physical devastation, and catastrophic multiple organ failures.

This is the story of that nightmare. Through it, I hope both to enlighten those of you less than familiar with marrow harvesting about the rationale for and steps involved in the delicate process, and to describe to all of you the potential repercussions inherent to extracting cells from the deep recesses of human bones. More importantly, (and hopefully without too large a dose of melodrama), I hope to reassure any one of you who end up in circumstances similar to ours that God does indeed send you enough miracles—in the form of minor medical surprises, thoughtful prayers from people you don't even know, and ever-closer relationships with both your friends and family—to help you trudge through each day until the whole situation is over.

Please be forewarned: this is not a detective story. It is an already verbally confessed-to fact that some break in sterilization during the harvest started my wife upon her nightmarish path. Nor is this story simply a condemnation of the marrow donor program in general. Too much good occurs–30,000 transplants per year worldwide with a cure rate near 80%, depending upon the stage of the offending disease–as a result of the program's efforts to declare it flawed because of a single failure point. Instead, this is simply a "quandary" story: not my wife's, not the doctors', but mine.

I am convinced that, given the opportunity to donate marrow all over again, my wife–just like almost every other past, present, and potential donor I have spoken to–would jump at the chance. The opportunity to improve the lot of someone without any hope left would undoubtedly and forever outweigh the slim possibility of something going wrong. The opportunity to save some father's or mother's or child's life by donating marrow is just too simple to resist: marrow harvesting is done on an out-patient basis and requires only the injection of two needles into the donor's pelvic bones. And, as I hinted at before, it is very difficult to out-run what is seen by most donors as an undeniable sign from God. (Matching types in each of the six tests requires beating odds of more than 20,000 to 1.) No, I have no doubt that, if she could have recovered completely, my wife would have immediately called the American Red Cross Marrow Donor Program and asked to be matched against another recipient as soon as physically possible. The quandary is definitely not hers.

No, the quandary is mine. For I do not think I could go along silently with her decision this time. Knowing what I know now, I would have questioned her about every step in the process when she came home with her "wonderful" news. I would have tried the logical argument that there is a very reasonable chance that the marrow she parted with would not actually cure anything. I believe I would have even tried to draw the line somewhere else: Do it to me, doctor, if you must, but please leave my family alone. Unfortunately, all my arguments and logic would have never (and probably should have never) changed her mind.

What stating those arguments and logic openly might have changed, though, was my attitude. Once I retired from submarine duty, Lina and I spent a lot of time talking in detail about finances and family and vacations and house repairs and even living wills, but we never spent much time on an apparently small thing like what it meant to sign up for the American Red Cross Marrow Donor program. By the time I thought to start those discussions, Lina had already been matched, leaving no civilized or Christian way for her or us to back out. So, I was both unprepared and angry when my wife finally slipped into a coma. I spent just as much time questioning the doctors and nurses as I did enlisting their help, which is just something you cannot afford to do in that type of situation.

I am writing this story, then, to ready you. Before you are forced to sit in the hospital visitor's area, waiting for the doctors to finish so that you can take your loved one home after the harvest, realize that this procedure is not as simple as getting a vaccination or having a tooth pulled. Bone marrow transplantation is truly a miraculous medical godsend, but it is not without its dangers. If, however, you've read about the procedure and talked about its possible repercussions beforehand, you can, at least, be ready for the worst. Then, when your harvest actually comes off without a hitch, you can toss off those anticipated worries, breathe easy, and laugh wholeheartedly at your good fortune…

… until you get your next match letter from the American Red Cross Marrow Donor Program.

LEUKEMIA

Perhaps. Perhaps it had been there since conception, coded into the genetic blueprint the mother and father had fused into the embryo. Perhaps it had appeared during the initial stages of pregnancy, a seemingly inconsequential glitch during a routine fetal cell division. Perhaps it had occurred sometime later, a hardly noticeable chemical or radioactive impulse, which irrevocably harmed a single stem cell deep inside the bone marrow. Or perhaps, all three together had caused his leukemia; to date, no one knows whether this diabolical disease is the result of abnormal heredity, nurture, or nature.

Leukemia: a condition of extreme leukocytosis. Leukocytosis: an over-abundance of leukocytes. (In Latin, "leukos" means white and "cyte" means cell; the word leukocyte is used in English to denote white blood cells.) Leukocytes: the body's first line of defense against illness and injury. Bottom line: leukemia is another example of the danger of too much of a good thing.

The recipient-to-be of my wife's marrow was a forty-one year-old Australian male suffering from that horrible disease. (For security purposes, we were told nothing else about him until one year after the transfusion was completed). His real name was Santo Caratozzolo; he was an Italian-born father of three–Shaun, Sandi, and Candice–living with his wife, Diane, in Perth, Australia. By the time Lina was identified as a potential savior, Santo's leukemia had already stricken him near death.

One of the reasons leukemia is so devastating both physically and emotionally is because it is a disease of the blood. The same blood which courses unseen, unfelt, and for the most part, unrecognized throughout our entire body. The same blood which delivers food to every single one of our seventy-five trillion cells. The same blood which produces over three million new cells each second. To find, diagnose, and treat something you rarely see, something which is everywhere, and something which reproduces itself with viral-like rapidity is a daunting task.

The blood that travels along our arteries, veins, and capillaries is about one-half water, one-half red blood cells, and less than one one-thousandth white blood cells. We originally get our blood through the umbilical cord from our mothers. Once organs like our spleen and liver grow into recognizable objects, they begin to produce large, specialized cells called stem cells. Stem cells are different than most other cells in our bodies. When most cells divide, they produce exact, duplicate copies of themselves; when stem cells divide, they eventually produce something different than themselves: red or white blood cells. After month five of the pregnancy, our skeletons have enlarged enough for the stem cells to migrate into the bone marrow which, from that point on, makes the marrow the predominate location for blood cell formation.

The red blood cells produced are essentially worker drones: they are made by the trillions, have no brain (nucleus), and die after traveling about 700 miles in 120 days. The white blood cells, on the other hand, are rather specialized machines. There are actually five different types–neutrophils, lymphocytes, monocytes, eosinophils, and basophils –which each combat infection, illness, or injury in their own special way. Though there is only one white blood cell for every 1000 red blood cells, these nucleus-laden cells can be very rapidly made, transported, and sacrificed for the good of the body.

In order to produce white blood cells, the stem cells inside your marrow must divide into four different types of cells. Stem cells become blast cells. Blast cells become myelocytes. Myelocytes become band cells. Finally, band cells become white blood cells and leak into the blood vessels to start circulating. You are considered normal as long as less than 5% of the cells inside a sample of your bone marrow are stuck in the blast cell phase.

That was Santo's problem. The number of blast cells in his marrow had skyrocketed. He was making enough blast cells, but those blast cells were not maturing. (The reasons for this blast-cell-inability-to-mature are currently not well understood. Abnormal stem cells, or incorrect maturation hormone application, or any one of a hundred other reasons could cause it.) Since the blast cells were not maturing, they were basically prohibited from leaking into the bloodstream.

Fewer white blood cells in circulation result in a decreased capability to ward off infection and illness. When finally there are no white blood cells in circulation, even minor colds become deadly. The excess blast cells in the marrow are not usually the actual cause of death; most people who are afflicted with leukemia simply cannot stave off any infection, no matter how minor it seems.

Santo had a type of leukemia called acute lymphocytic leukemia (ALL). This type of leukemia is characterized by an abundance of immature lymphocytes in the marrow. It is called "acute" because, once started, the disease progresses extremely rapidly. It is also sometimes called childhood leukemia because, by itself, ALL accounts for an amazing 85% of all leukemia cases in children.

The good news concerning this form of leukemia is for children: current medical advances can help force 80% to 90% of all childhood ALL cases into remission for three years or more; 75% of those will eventually be completely cured. The bad news is for patients over fifteen years of age: even if the disease's advance can be halted medically, most will survive less than two years.

Assuming you catch it early enough, though, ALL is actually treatable. Once the paleness, weakness, easy bleeding or bruising, enlarged organs (lymph nodes, spleen, or liver), fever, bone or joint pain, or frequent infections point the doctor toward the correct diagnosis, medical science has developed a rather aggressive course toward wellness. It is not, however, an easy course. To repair the white blood cell development process, doctors cannot simply feed the patient a couple antibiotics or remove a pint or two of blood. They must instead completely destroy every stem cell inside every bone in the body and bring in new ones from elsewhere, in the hope that what was inhibiting maturation was not so much a glitch in the body or brain or hormones, but simply a set of bad stem cells gone berserk.

Stem-cell destruction comes in the form of high-dose chemotherapy and full-body radiation events for ten full days. One option sometimes employed is to spread out four huge doses of a drug like Cytoxan and four thirty-minute total body X-rays over those ten days. The side effects of this treatment cycle are devastating; there is the distinct possibility of nausea, vomiting, abnormal fluid retention, blood in the urine, loss of hair, heart damage, internal hemorrhaging, skin rash, diarrhea, liver damage, severe pneumonia, long-term sterility, and even cataracts.

At the end of the chemotherapy and radiation therapy combination, the patient is left without stem cells, white blood cells, an immune system, or resistance to infection. As he or she sits defenseless and nearly dead in total isolation inside intensive care, two critical issues remain:

- Are all the offending cells gone?
- How soon will the pristine savior cells take to get here?

If nothing were done to the patient, if no new stem cells were transplanted, there would be at most two days left to worry before certain death. During those two days then, the two critical issues above quickly go from quiet questions to exclamations to pleas to prayers.

Santo's stem cell transfusion was indeed delivered in time. After making the flight from California to Australia, the cells were quickly injected into Santo's circulation. It would take two to four weeks to see a rise in his white blood cell count, signaling that Lina's stem cells had grafted to the marrow and resumed production. In keeping with everything else which happened as a result of Lina's harvest, though, the stem cells never really had the chance to graft.

Within weeks of the bone marrow transplant, Santo was back in the hospital, suffering from the same sequence of illnesses and infections which would eventually plague Lina. Within months of the bone marrow transplant, Santo would be dead. My wife never even had a chance to meet him.

PERFECT LIVES

There are currently over three million kind souls who have volunteered to donate their marrow wherever and whenever it is needed. That means there are over three million potential donor stories to be told.

Most of the American stories are summarized and tabulated in the National Marrow Donor Program database. As a part of this database, my wife's story was actually rather average:

- At the time she submitted her application, she was 35 years old. The average American blood donor is between 30 and 50 years of age.
- We have always been "modestly" middle-class. According to the American Red Cross blood donor statistics, the average donor also has "above-average" income.
- Being white and female is also standard fare. 85% of blood donors are white, and 47% are female.

In spite of that apparent "average-ness", our lives before the donation were decidedly not middle-of-the-road. Instead, I would, without reservation, characterize our lives as perfect.

We were a Navy family. In fact, we were a Naval Submariner family. For those of you unfamiliar with the rigors of that type of naval life, suffice it to say that, for twenty years, I spent at least nine out of every twelve months under water hiding from all of civilization, and the other three months on land trying to make up for lost time. Though most would tend to see such a home-again, away-again lifestyle as detrimental to family strength, it actually offered us a great opportunity to become incredibly close.

A submariner family was usually a hit-or-miss proposition. A life that involved months completely incommunicado followed by a few weeks of constant interaction is rather strange. A life which involved many months of mom serving as both mom and dad, followed by intermittent periods of dad trying to take back his role, is rather difficult. Understandably, many wives and many husbands could not adapt to that type of environment. They either ended up divorced or stayed together until death.

Fortunately, we had no such problems. I loved my calling; it was not only challenging, but also was patriotically fulfilling. More importantly, my career choice afforded Lina the opportunity to play the "Supermom" she had always strived to be: single parent from sun-up to sun-down, dental office manager five days a week, PTA board member, Little League mom, Sunday School teacher, choir member, and Girl's Club leader. Every time I surfaced, I found a lovely woman who was, at the same time, hurried, harried, and happy. (One time, I even found her two and a half months from delivery of a child. It was pretty amazing–waving good-bye to a flat belly, and saying hello to a tummy-kicking baby–but that sort of surprise always made life exciting.)

The bumps in the road never seemed to faze her and, with me gone, those bumps had the propensity to become rather significant. Take, for example, the standard day-at-the-beach situation. In most normal families, mom and dad dump the kids into the minivan for an uneventful day of boogie boarding; the only problems encountered usually involve not enough sunscreen or too much sand. With one parent 20,000 leagues under the sea, however, there were several twists to our version of the story. "Wondermom" decides that eight kids (ours plus all the nieces plus everybody's best friend), sand chairs, towels, a radio, an ice chest, and boogie boards is a reasonable load for the Bronco, so off she treks. At the end of the day, she brings everybody back to our house to rinse off the layer of beach they brought back with them. Finally, after taking care of everyone else, Lina dumps the towels in the washer and heads for a well-deserved shower.

Five minutes later, pandemonium owns the house. One of our nieces is screaming, "Fire! Fire! FIRE!" while banging on the shower door. Instinctively, Lina scoops up a towel in one hand and the niece in the other, and races to get everyone out of the house.

If our lives truly weren't so blessed, things could have become rather tragic rather quickly. But, since God has never actually given us more than we could handle, the "fire" wasn't really a fire; it was, instead, just our washer (on its last legs) belching smoke. So, Lina crawls behind the machine to unplug the beast. It is only after she is basically stuck behind the machine that our daughter, Dina, remembers to tell mom that she had called 911 when the chaos had first started. Lina drops her head; she has no doubt as to what must happen next.

Sure enough, the fire truck arrives immediately, and three hunks of firemen (her words) come running into the house to find not a fire, but a mom (with only terry cloth covering her birthday suit) hiding behind a dead washing machine. Never has the world seen such a red-colored blush; never have eight kids laughed at one Kool-Aid mom for so long.

Most of our lives were just like that: minor catastrophes that ended in some humorous twist. Even when things really did go wrong, however, some higher force prevented them from going horribly wrong. Lina's mall story is an excellent example of that.

In December of 1982, we were in the midst of moving from San Francisco to San Diego. "We" is probably a misnomer, because only Lina was there to oversee the move; I had left early to take the sub down south after an extensive modification, and the kids had left early to spend some time with Lina's parents. So, Lina was forced once again to single-handedly sort our belongings, watch the packers, and pass the departure-from-Navy-housing white glove inspection.

Faced with all that, Lina decided instead to go shopping for the kids' Christmas presents. She went to a mall in the town of Richmond, California, and spent the evening ensuring that her undersea Santa Claus husband would look like a hero to her kids on Christmas day.

As she got ready to leave (filled to the brim with presents), Lina struggled to get the key in the car door. Her next sensation, however, surprised her: she felt the air in her lungs rushing out as she hit the cold asphalt hard. The presents then went flying.

The force of the fall gave Lina little time to collect her thoughts: explosion, earthquake, heart attack? Before she could decide which one, the large man in the ski mask who had tackled her jumped on her and rolled her onto her back. Lina screamed in quick recognition of her predicament; the man dealt a crushing blow across her face in response. "Another sound and I'll kill you!" were the only words he said. Between that and the knife he held at her neck, Lina was forced to meekly comply.

As he ripped at her blouse, Lina realized how deserted a mall parking lot can be. She truly had no recourse to stop the behemoth straddling her waist. So, God saved the day. He sent an angel (in the form of a seventy year-old man running and screaming and waving his arms) to stop the madness. Slowly, the would-be rapist, realizing that he had been seen, gathered up most of the packages from the ground and slithered back into the darkness.

As a crowd of people gathered, Lina eventually picked herself up off the ground and tried to compose herself once more. After thanking God about a million times, she turned to thank her Good Samaritan. In keeping with the eeriness of this story, the white knight had, of course, disappeared just as quickly as he had appeared, never to be thanked for saving not just one life, but the livelihood of an entire family as well.

Similar (though thankfully less dramatic) stories always filled our lives. Somehow, though, we always managed to have enough money, better than expected health, and less than the average number of family catastrophes.

And since, to those who much is given, much is expected, we usually tried to do what we could for others. So, seven years after her initial application, when the American Red Cross Marrow Donor Program called excitedly to say, "You're a solid six! Can we get your marrow immediately?" there was truly nothing we could respond with except, "But, of course."

Matching

It is amazingly simple to volunteer your bone marrow on demand. In the United States, you first call the National Marrow Donor Program at 1-800-MARROW-2, listen to the automated selection menu, and clearly state your name and address when asked. Within a week, a brochure describing the National Marrow Donor Program arrives in your mail box. (You can also do these steps on-line by surfing the National Marrow Donor Program web site at www.marrow.org.)

Besides answering some generic questions—what is bone marrow?, who can donate?, etc.—and describing some tug-at-your-heartstrings personal interest stories, the National Marrow Donor Program brochure also contains a list of the country's donor center phone numbers. Once you call the donor center nearest you, their operators inform you about becoming a volunteer donor and about the actual steps in the donation process. Then, they send you a set of consent forms and do a cursory medical history check on you. (You cannot donate marrow if you are under 18 or over 60; have a history of cancer, diabetes, heart disease, or heart attack; are greatly overweight; or are at high risk for contraction of AIDS or HIV.)

Once you complete the consent and history forms, you walk into the donor center and give a small amount of blood. This blood is tested to determine your Human Leukocyte Antigen (HLA) type; that type is then entered into the National Marrow Donor Program registry. At this point, you have successfully completed the bone marrow donation volunteer application process.

Perhaps it is so amazingly simple to volunteer your bone marrow because God has made it so amazingly difficult for anyone else to actually use your bone marrow. The HLA system inside your body is so intricate and so difficult to replicate that it truly makes successful bone marrow transplantation nearly impossible.

To fully appreciate the HLA system, we must first delve back into a discussion of the white blood cell, specifically the lymphocyte. The majority of lymphocytes are created in an organ called the thymus (right above the heart and right behind the sternum) and are, therefore, called T-cells. Their job is to act like the body's Passover Angels and destroy every damaged cell they find.

Every cell in your body has a number of HLA proteins inside to assist in damage control. If a cell is normal, the HLA protein inside that cell has only one job: it grabs things called peptides from the inside of the cell and places them onto the outside of the cell for release to the rest of the body. As the HLA-peptide molecule sits on the cell membrane, T-cells in the blood arrive to check it out.

The T-cell and HLA-peptide molecule are basically puzzle pieces; only if they are made exactly for each other will they connect correctly. If the connection is indeed nominal, the T-cell will quickly disconnect, pass over the good cell, and continue on its way.

It is only when the cell is damaged or poisoned that the true magic begins. In this case, the HLA protein begins its secondary tasking: it grabs either an incorrectly formed peptide (created if the cell is damaged) or the offending poison, and carries these "antigens" outside the cell. As the HLA-antigen molecule sits on the cell membrane, T-cells once again arrive. This time, though, the HLA-antigen and T-cell puzzle pieces do not match up, and alarms begin to go off. Quickly, the T-cell divides itself into "killer" T-cells; those killers will either rupture the cell membrane, inject a truly deadly poison directly into the cell, or activate genes in the cell nucleus which convince the cell to commit suicide.

The system is nearly flawless. It is also very individualized: your T-cells and HLA proteins are specifically made only for each other.

That is a key issue in transplantation. Say you receive a kidney from a generous donor. The kidney is perfectly healthy, each cell is releasing peptides as it should, and perfectly normal HLA proteins are carrying all those peptides to the outside of each cell. The problem with this perfect scenario is that, if the HLA proteins inside the transplanted kidney are not the same as the ones you were born with, your T-cells will drop by, not connect properly, and set out to kill everything in their path. Quickly, your blood will utterly destroy the Samaritan's kidney.

The situation is even worse with bone marrow transplants. If the donor and receiver are not perfectly matched, not only will the HLA proteins be different, but so will all the T-cells produced by the new marrow. It does not truly matter which of the two puzzle pieces do not match: if either the HLA protein or T-cell do not fit correctly into one another, the T-cell will be forced to destroy the cell with "bad" HLA. And, so it will go with every cell in every organ in your body: your newly formed blood will declare them all foreign and set out to kill them all. With incorrectly matched marrow, you quickly die from the inside out.

The important proteins with respect to transplantation are called HLA-A, HLA-B, and HLA-DR. (Each of the three works inside a different type of cell.) You get one of each protein type from your mom and one from your dad, meaning that most cells in your body have one of six HLA protein types running peptides and antigens out of the cell.

Since there are many different types of each HLA protein, medical personnel have developed quick, efficient methods to determine which specific two of the HLA-A, HLA-B, and HLA-DR protein types you have. A very small drop of your collected blood (full of T-cells) is placed on a slide containing separated samples of every kind of HLA-A protein currently known. Quickly, your T-cells kill every sample except two; those are your HLA-A types. Likewise, your T-cells kill off all but two of the HLA-B and

HLA-DR samples. At the end of all this killing, your genetic HLA coding is completely known.

If you need something like marrow, trying to get a complete six-of-six match to your genetic coding is incredibly difficult. Identical twins have it easy; they automatically match on all six HLA proteins. Parents and children share at least three of the six (because the child actually received three proteins from each parent). Since siblings get their HLA proteins from the same two-person pool, the odds of matching three is about 12%, and the odds of matching all six is about 2%. If, however, you are not lucky enough to have an identical twin to get you your marrow, and if your parents, brothers, and sisters cannot help either, finding a perfect stranger whose HLA's match yours perfectly becomes truly like searching for a needle in a gigantic haystack.

Scientists are continually attempting to isolate new types of HLA proteins. Currently, they have either successfully or have nearly successfully isolated 19 different HLA-A proteins, 39 different HLA-B proteins, and 14 different HLA-DR proteins. Those numbers may not seem that huge, but when combined together, they help create rather remote possibilities.

To demonstrate that, assume each of those proteins is a different lottery ball, and there are balls separated into six different selection bins: 19 numbered A balls in the first selection bin, 19 numbered A balls in the second bin, 39 numbered B balls in the third, 39 B balls in the fourth, and 14 DR balls each in the fifth and sixth. Now, assume that you are the patient in need of matched marrow, so you choose balls first and come out with A-6, A-8, B-4, B-39, DR-1, and DR-13.

You replace the balls and ask your best friend to try to pull out the same set of six. Quickly, the laws of probability take hold: your friend has a 2-in-19 chance of pulling the A-6 or A-8 ball from the first bin, a 1-in-19 chance of pulling the other A ball from the second bin, a 2-in-39 chance of pulling one of the B balls from the third bin, a 1-in-39 chance of pulling the other B ball from the fourth bin, a 2-in-14 chance of pulling one of the right DR balls from the fifth bin, and a 1-in-14 chance of pulling the other DR ball from the sixth bin. The total probability is the product of all these individual probabilities, and works out to 1-in-13,452,484! Which means you had better have over 13 million best friends (i.e., nearly everyone who currently lives in Australia) or you had better get real lucky with the friends you have!

As of 1995, though, you only had three million "best friends" scattered throughout the world, registered as potential marrow donors in their country's donor databases. It would take five to ten more applicants for each one there is now to give all those who require marrow a decent chance at finding a donor.

Amazingly, Lina was an "unrelated six-of-six" match for Santo. She quickly came to believe that her success at overcoming those 1-in-13-million-plus odds to help Santo was more than blind luck; she saw it instead as the result of divine intervention, a direct message from God which simply could not be ignored. Had I chosen to, it would have been difficult to argue otherwise.

Once the database discovers a match, the local donor center calls the volunteer donor. It is at this point that the hard questions are asked: Are you still medically eligible to donate? Are you still willing to donate?

While those questions are being asked and answered, another sample of your blood is taken and sent in for confirmatory testing. In confirmatory testing, the new sample is examined by the center which will actually inject the collected marrow, in an attempt to ensure that the volunteer's donor center correctly typed the initial sample.

Given yes answers and no typing errors, the donor is provided a counseling session (where, though it probably would not change things, the dangers associated with donation are given much less air time than the wonders derived from donation) and a cursory physical examination. If all results are positive, the date and place for the marrow harvest are finally scheduled.

Wednesday, December 11, 1996. Lina's day.

HARVESTING

December 11, 1996

I awoke to a gentle rain dripping from the eaves. Pulling back the curtain, it was still dark.

"Can you have anything to eat, honey?" I asked.

With a smile, she just shook her head no. The harvest was scheduled for 11:00 A.M., and Lina was not permitted food or drink until after it was finished.

Lina and I were usually up early, so getting up at 5:00 A.M. to get ready for the harvest was not that different from most days. As always, we were trying to be quiet, so we would not wake up the rest of the household–my daughter, Dina, her husband, Bryan, and their son, Rilley–who had moved in with us while saving to buy their own home.

Downstairs, I saw that Bryan was already off to work, and I poured a cup of coffee from the fresh pot he had left. Though it was still two weeks away, it did indeed seem like Christmas with the cold rain falling, the house full of Lina's decorations, and the heavy scent of the pine tree in the family room. Life was good already and Lina was about to make someone's Christmas just a little better with her priceless gift of life!

Although the harvesting was to be done at a hospital that was just seventeen miles away in nearby Orange County, the Los Angeles area traffic ruled our schedule. At a snail's pace, we crawled through a parking lot facetiously called the I-5 freeway. The already heavy traffic was slowed even further by the steady, soft rain.

With the windshield wipers slowly doing their dance, Lina stared out of her window at Disneyland. "I wonder how many people would still go there on a day like today?"

"I don't know, but I'll bet the lines aren't too long for the rides!" I replied.

The main lounge to the hospital was beautiful. Tall, green-tinted glass windows focused life-giving light onto the large potted palms. The reception area looked more like that of a fine hotel than a hospital. Overall, the whole place seemed to reflect the above average income of the Orange County area of Southern California.

The lounge seemed a little busy for that time of the morning. Our receptionist at the check-in desk apologized as she fumbled with admission forms. "I've been gone for six weeks, and you're my first admission this morning." We were patient; Lina just smiled.

Soon, Lina was off to be "prepped" for the harvest. As the nurse was taking Lina's blood pressure, she explained the procedure one more time. The representative from the National Marrow Donor Program stopped by to reassure us and to ask Lina if she had any changes. We handed her a box of chocolates and a card to be sent to the recipient along with the marrow. In the card, Lina expressed her prayer for God's healing touch on the gift she was about to give.

That was truly the point of no return. The recipient's own marrow and immune system had been depleted to nothing by chemotherapy and radiation treatments. If Lina's priceless marrow did not get to him now, he would die in a matter of days. That was made very clear to us. The enormous responsibility of this man's fate was dropped on Lina like a colossal weight hung around her shoulders. How could she or anyone have backed out at this point?

Lina signed the final consent forms, and my angel of life was wheeled without me through the double doors of the operating room, where only a select few are allowed to go and no layman are allowed to observe. Having full trust in their quality of training and their level of professional skill, I questioned nothing about this "simple" procedure. Her smile, her big blue eyes, and a little wave over her shoulder were the last I saw of Lina, not knowing that, within a matter of hours, our lives would be horribly changed forever by microorganisms so small that they cannot be seen with the naked eye.

A quick check of my day planner and I was off. In my brain, organized by twenty years of submarine schedules and procedures, I tried to squeeze the most out of every day. "Waste not a minute that could be productive work, so I could spend the best of times with my family," was my motto. I knew that Lina would not be back into the recovery room until 2:00 P.M. That would give me enough time to attend an 11:00 A.M. funeral for a dear friend, spend about an hour at work, and still make it back to the hospital before Lina could even miss me.

Outside the recovery room, I stared at my watch as if that would make the time go by faster. At 2:00 P.M., Lina was still not out. A nurse came by to tell me that sometimes, with some patients, it takes a little more than a couple hours to finish the harvest. A little longer turned out to be an hour; finally, at 3:00 P.M., Lina was out of the operating room and into recovery. I had to wait another hour to see her. At 4:00 P.M., Lina was responding about as well as a drunken sailor. Her speech was slurred, and she smiled a lot.

"Are you sore?" I asked.

"I think so," she stammered.

I assured her that everything was okay. The nursing staff told me that, if she continued to respond well, she could go home that very night! Great!

At 8:00 P.M., Lina was alert. Sore, but ready to go home. The representative from the National Marrow Donor Program, at the end of a very long day for her, stopped by again. She brought us a thank-you card, a stuffed koala with a Santa's cap, and a gold heart-shaped lapel pin; all gifts sent by the recipient. The gifts we received were much like the gifts we sent: hand-written, full of blessings, and (in keeping with National Marrow Donor Program rules) devoid of names and signatures.

A ride in the wheelchair to the door, and then Lina and I walked ever so slowly, arm in arm, through the parking lot in the cold night air. The sky was (uncharacteristically for Los Angeles) clear and full of stars once the rain clouds drifted away.

In the car, Lina studied the two gifts and card from her recipient. Could the stuffed koala really have meant that Lina's marrow had gone all the way to Australia? Maybe not. The recipient's family could have bought that koala anywhere. I was sure that that little guy could have been sitting on the shelf of a gift shop in Cleveland, Ohio just a few days ago, for all that mattered!

But, Lina looked ever more closely at the back of the thank-you card. There was no Hallmark® or American Greetings® on the back of this one. It was printed by a company in Australia!

The little gold heart-shaped lapel pin was also mounted on a holding card. On the back of that card, it said, "Made in Sydney, Australia"! It didn't take Sherlock Holmes to figure where her marrow had gone.

As we looked again into the night sky, Lina and I prayed Godspeed for her gift now in flight to Santo.

THE NEXT DAY

December 12, 1996

Lina slept well through the night. She was up and raring to go just like every other morning. I asked her several times if she was sure that she wanted to go to work. She looked at me as though I was crazy. "Look honey, I'm sore just like they said I'd be, but I'm no wimp! Now quit worrying about me, and you get to work yourself!" So off to work I went.

My day at work was busy, since I was trying to make up for my lost time from the day before. Around 12:30 in the afternoon, I called Lina to see how she was doing. I was completely surprised when the ladies at the office told me she had gone home in extreme pain. I called home, but there was no answer. Maybe she had stopped off at the pharmacy to fill a prescription for painkillers. Lina worked only five minutes from home. "Well, I shouldn't worry," I consoled myself, "I'm sure everything is all right; it always is."

2:00 P.M. Still no answer at home.

3:00 P.M. No answer. Now, I was worried. Her mother had not heard from her, and none of her friends had either. I called Dina at work. She reassured me that everything was all right. Dina also works five minutes away from home; she told me that she would go straight to the house and check on her mom as soon as she got off work.

4:15 P.M. Dina called me. "Dad, you need to get home as soon as you can! I found Mom upstairs in your bed. She is hurting bad! She can't move her right leg and she has a high fever."

For the next two hours, I did battle with the L.A. traffic while burning up my cell phone. (I work forty-five miles from home. On a good day, it takes me ninety minutes to slog through traffic.) Dina and I were talking with the doctors and the pharmacist. Dina left her mother only to grab a quick prescription for a pretty potent pain-killer called Vicodin.

Once I got the car in the driveway, I flew through the front door and up the stairs. There lay Lina crying in pain, a washcloth on her forehead and Dina at her side. "Dad, I don't think she should take anymore of these." Dina was holding up the prescription bottle. "She has been eating them like candy, and they don't seem to help."

I quickly jumped on the phone with the doctor again; he was sure that she was just sorer than most people. I tried to explain that I knew my wife, and that she was not prone to bouts of unnecessary whining. Whatever it was that was hurting her, I screamed, it must have been very bad. She could not stand up! She was losing the use of her right leg! She could not move without crying! Finally, to silence my incessant demands and pleas, the hospital agreed to let me bring her in.

My poor Lina was in such pain that simply trying to help her into a sitting position brought streams of tears and mumbled begging not to move her. In a desperate attempt to get her downstairs and into the car, I scooped her up in my arms like a newlywed groom crossing the threshold. Lina cried out in pain and told me she couldn't do it. As I laid her back down softly onto the bed, I told Lina that I was calling for an ambulance. She just shook her head no. I was not sure though if she could really think rationally with that level of pain and with the painkillers clouding her mind.

After ten minutes of small gentle movements, we finally moved her to the edge of the bed in a sitting position. With Bryan under one arm, me under the other, and Dina supporting in the back, we took about a million baby steps to the top of the stairs. It took us forty-five minutes to make it down the stairs and into the car.

Our innocent little grandson, Rilley, just didn't understand all the consternation. "Is Oma all right? Is Oma sick? Does Oma have a boo-boo foot?"

104°F fever, excruciating pain, and paralysis. Not exactly the type of reaction one would expect after a "normal" harvest. Things went so bad so quickly that Lina and I were headed to the emergency room less than 27 hours after her initial discharge.

Once in the car, Lina, like the princess with a pea under her mattress, felt every little bit of movement on an otherwise smoothly paved street. At the hospital, the nurse and I did the same slow dance getting Lina from the car into the wheelchair. From there, she was wheeled directly into an examination room. The emergency room doctor was pretty sure that Lina's right sciatic nerve had been disturbed and thought that was the cause of her excruciating pain. He told me that the nerve could have easily been brushed during the harvesting.

(In retrospect, what should have seemed strange is this: if the nerve-brushing hypothesis was true, you would think that she would have felt that much pain right away during her recovery. But what did I know? They were the doctors. They should have known. Shouldn't they?)

The doctor started Lina on a morphine drip to control the pain. He ran a complete blood count as a standard routine, and called for admission orders. Lina was admitted into the hospital around 1:00 A.M.

By late morning, Lina's lab tests were coming back. The doctor started her on a course of antibiotics. He was puzzled at the amount of pain she was in. I didn't care. My concern was much simpler: "How long before you cure her, and when will she be well enough to go home?"

I ll Be Home For Christmas!

December 17, 1996

The most expeditious place to extract marrow from a donor is to take it from inside the hip. To do that, the operating team turns the donor face down and goes through the skin near the small of the back.

Injecting a sharp object directly into any bone is very painful. Deadening the nerves with a general anesthetic will fool the body into ignoring the pain short-term, but once the drugs wear off, the long-term anguish due to the bone-stabbing will basically feel something akin to being kicked by a rather large horse at very close range.

Since you can only get a tiny bit of marrow from each section of bone, donating marrow usually requires injections into about twenty-five sections of each hipbone. (Thankfully, it doesn't take twenty-five injections through the skin, since you can leave the needle below the skin throughout the procedure.) Doctors use a tool called a trocar to repeatedly break into the hipbone.

According to the dictionary, the trocar is a "sharp-pointed surgical instrument used to puncture a body cavity for fluid aspiration." Think of the trocar as a razor-sharp soda straw, which the doctor slides through your skin, through the hard outer layer of your hip bone, and into the soft, mushy center of the bone where the marrow is made.

If the trocar were exactly like a straw, it would get plugged up with skin and tissue and bone well before it got to the marrow. So, the trocar is made with a sheath that covers the end of the needle. Once the doctor actually hits marrow, that sheath (which, to be perfectly accurate, is the actual trocar) gets pulled back, leaving a needle through which the marrow can then be sucked out.

Unfortunately, the marrow around the needle has a consistency something like Slurpee®; once you suck a little out through the straw, the area around the needle basically runs "dry." To get any more marrow, you have to re-sheath the needle, pull it back out of the bone, find a new place to put it in, push it through to the marrow, and suck out the next Slurpeeful. Twenty-five times more and they finally leave your hip alone.

The trocar used to extract marrow from Lina's right hip was contaminated with a staphylococcus (staph) bacterium. As it made its way into the core of Lina's body, it left little staph deposits under her skin, in her blood, on her bone, and alongside her marrow.

Scientists have known about the round bacterium called coccus for over 100 years. Alone, each coccus is a pretty harmless animal; it is only when a large number of these cocci join that monstrous infections can occur. When the cocci hook together to form a train, that train is called streptococcus bacteria. This is the culprit behind a number of rather benign illnesses like strep throat; streptococcus infections can usually be eradicated completely through the use of penicillin.

When the cocci hook together to form a glob, the mass is called staphylococcus bacteria. Unlike its well-ordered counterpart, staph both causes pretty catastrophic illnesses and does not respond well to anything but the strongest antibiotics.

We live in a world full of staph. The goal of each of those little staph particles is to find a warm, wet, dark place–i.e., deep inside your body–to call home. Thankfully, our skin, nose hairs, saliva, and tear ducts keep most staph on the outside and, therefore, ineffective. It is only when those molecules do get inside that they begin to have damaging effects.

If you get a superficial cut, do not bother to clean it, and allow the staph on your skin to enter just under your skin, the staph will do one of three things: 1) it may find a hair follicle and create an inflamed, painful boil full of thick yellow pus; 2) it may form a patch of tiny blisters which break to expose a patch of red, moist, weeping skin called impetigo; or 3) it may simply get red and swell into a disease called cellulitis, also forming red lines which run from nearby lymph nodes to the infected area.

If the staph makes it into your bloodstream, it is quickly attracted to your lymph nodes, heart valves, lungs, kidneys, and brain. Once it arrives at its desired location, it disintegrates the local tissue and molds that tissue into a pus-filled abscess. The abscess will (especially in the lungs and kidneys) infect the area, cause some local inflammation, and hinder organ operation until it induces organ failure.

Finally, if the staph infection ever finds bone, it will simply bore a hole there by eating everything in its path. The telltale abscess usually lodges itself right next to the inflamed bone.

Most incidences of staph infections begin outside on the skin and proceed inside to the blood and bones, so you can usually see that you have staph well before it does any real internal damage. Lina's infection was so dangerous because it went just the opposite way; it started in her bones, found its way into her bloodstream, and finally worked up toward the surface. Lina's staph had scorched a wide swath through her well before it showed itself.

It was a full three days after the harvest before a blood test indicated that Lina had contracted a staph infection. Because nothing out of the ordinary had happened yet, her doctor surmised that the staph had simply snuck under the skin near her right hip. The standard procedure doctors take in that case is to try to beat the staph back with a long-duration penicillin series. Since normal intravenous (IV) lines usually have to be replaced every seventy-two hours, they had to install a long-lasting Picc line, instead.

Think of a Picc line as a long, under-skin IV. (Picc stands for Peripherally Inserted Central Catheter.) The doctor slides it into a vein—usually the one in your upper arm—and pushes the attached plastic tube along that vein until it gets near your collarbone. That means the tip is much closer to the "center" of your body, so injecting penicillin through that tube is a very effective means of administering antibiotics. A battery-operated pump held in a pack around your waist pushes the medicine through the long tube and into your bloodstream.

Unfortunately, Picc lines are also very prone to clogging at the tip. So, Lina needed blood-thinning drugs to release the recurring clots, in addition to the morphine she was taking for the pain and the penicillin she was taking for the staph. This mixture of multiple drugs—and their unpredictable interactions—would soon become a constant part of Lina's life. Though I am not a doctor, I quickly began to believe this jumbled-drug therapy was doing little to improve, but much to exacerbate, Lina's health problems.

Once the Picc line was installed, the doctors attempted to figure out what other ills the staph had induced. There is a high risk of damage to the fragile heart valves when a heavy staph infection is running through your veins. So, later that same day, they did an echocardiogram to check the health of her heart valves. This scan is like the ultrasound done on expectant mothers. Since there is bone in front and in back and to the side of the heart, though, you cannot get an unobstructed view of it from outside the body. So, doctors place the ultrasonic device down the patient's throat, instead. This allows the sound waves to hit the heart and bounce back without being obstructed by the bony rib cage. Lina's echocardiogram showed one set of unaffected valves; another set was too difficult to see.

As if Lina had not had enough tests for the day, the doctors wanted to slip in just one more. This last test was a bone scan. By injecting a radioactive chemical into her hip, an X-ray taken of the hip right after would show any dead tissue as dark spots. Based on the results of this test, we finally discovered that there indeed was staph inhabiting Lina's right side.

All in all, though, it seemed as though everything was under control. The doctors had controlled her fever, and had found the staph infection that was causing the fever. Lina was on a good dose of the antibiotics via her PICC line, she could walk with the use of a walker, and she was itching to go home. "I'll be home for Christmas," was our theme, as we looked to a discharge date before the holidays were upon us. Thankfully, we made it home on the 21st of December, 1996.

Christmas was a little lean that year. With Lina out of work and me trying to juggle work and daily trips to the hospital, there was a constant wear on the savings account. In spite of that, the Christmas Eve service at church was just as beautiful as it was every year, even though Lina was missing from her spot in the choir loft. Unable to negotiate the steps in her walker or to stand for any appreciable length of time, Lina and I instead sat in the pew, singing our hearts out. As we praised God for sending us his Son, streams of tears ran down my angel's face.

At home, we opened gifts, as was our family's tradition, after the Christmas Eve service. Warm and happy around the tree with our children and grandson, we prayed a moment for a family we did not know, thousands of miles away in Australia. "Lord, if it is Your will, please heal him, and give comfort to his family on this holy night."

The idea that this might be the family's last Christmas together did not hinder our own family's celebration, but those concerns loomed large during Santo's family's holidays. Lina had but a single little infection to overcome. Santo still had to regenerate a whole new immune system to save his own life. Little did we know that the tempest in Lina's bones was gaining strength like a hurricane over warm water.

Before the Storm

January 24, 1997

It is hard, in retrospect, to fault anyone for what happened next. For, after our initial scare, Lina started to respond positively to her treatment. Her fever broke and the pain stopped, even when she started taking oral antibiotics. For a time, we all relaxed and marveled at our collective brilliance.

Forty-three days after her harvest (and on the day after she had finished her last dose of oral medicine), my wife's body ensured we would never make that mistake again. The pain came back hard. The staph levels in her blood skyrocketed.

On Friday, January 24th, 1997, Lina was back in the hospital with mirrored symptoms of when this all began. The next day, whole batteries of tests were conducted to get a better picture of what was going on. More radioactive "tagging" of the white blood cells, an X-ray of the hip, and a computed tomography (CT) scan were used to try to determine the exact location and magnitude of the infection. Right after all that, the doctors gave Lina Nafcillin—a very potent form of penicillin—through a newly installed Picc line.

Finally, that evening, the doctors put all the clues together, realized that the trocar must have been the smoking gun, and prepared to do the only thing possible when staph takes hold within the bone: cut it away. There were dark "honeycomb" images on the CT scan and X-ray which revealed damage much more extensive than they had previously believed. Surgery was scheduled for Thursday, January 30th. My reaction to all of this was, "Let's get it right, and let's get it all!"

Post surgery, the surgeon explained what he saw and what he did. The cut he made through Lina's right pelvic bone was an oval shape that he called a "window." In the very center of that window was the small hole through which the trocar had bored fifty-one days before. After lifting up the two-inch by four-inch window, the doctor observed a pocket of pus at the very point the trocar had entered into Lina's marrow. The damage to the inner bone was great. The weeks of antibiotics had not done much to arrest the spread of infection within her own life-giving marrow; there were just not enough avenues for the antibiotics to get back into the bone where it was needed. The debridement the surgeon did to remove the dead bone was extensive and required bone grafting to strengthen the rest of her pelvis. Lina's resulting incision was large and crescent-shaped, and went from waistline to leg-line. I never could have guessed beforehand just how large of an opening the doctor would need to get to her pelvis.

I expected this surgery to be the last hurdle that we would have to jump over. I figured that Lina would soon be improving by leaps and bounds. Unfortunately, that was not to be. In fact, Lina was very weak and vomiting everyday. For the first time, I started to become really concerned about just how sick she was. I thought, "Why does it seem that each day is just a little bit worse than the day before?"

By that time, I had developed a routine which allowed me to spend maximum time with Lina. I had basically moved into Lina's room. I stayed with her all day and helped the nurses attempt to feed her, bathe her, and change her gowns. The nurses kept Lina in a private room with a very large easy chair that laid out nearly flat to sleep in. So, at night when Lina went to sleep, I went to sleep in my big easy chair right next to her bed. The nurses were very good to me, too; they would bring me extra pillows and cover me with blankets. At 4:00 A.M. each morning, I would wake up and head for home. I would check the mailbox and send out the bills. I would change the message on the answering machine to update family and friends as to Lina's current condition, then shower and change into fresh clothes, and finally get back to the hospital in time for Lina's 6:00 A.M. blood draw.

It was during this early February hospital stay that one of the doctors first showed me how to read her lab report. From that point on, the doctors made sure I received a copy of her lab report daily. That ability alone helped me feel like I was part of the medical team charged with curing my wife's ills.

One day, in mid-February, our story took another turn for the worse. Eunice, our day nurse, was hanging a bag of honey-looking fluid to tap into Lina's IV.

"What's that?" I questioned.

"Albumin. It's pretty expensive stuff, too!" Eunice said, as she worked with the connection.

"Really? How much?" I asked. The thought of how much all this must be costing had never crossed my mind.

"I've been told about $300 a dose," Eunice said with a smirk. "It just keeps on adding up!"

Now I was beginning to wonder just how much this was costing. Was I going to be billed? I sat and wondered if any of the staff had any idea. Did I dare ask? Eunice came back into the room sometime later to check on Lina's IV.

"Well, what have you heard?" I asked her out of the blue.

"Heard?" she asked back, as she furrowed her brow.

"The cost of all this," I said quietly.

"Well, you didn't hear it from me, but rumor has it that your bill is close to a million already. I'm sure they want your wife to recuperate at home!"

As it turned out, Eunice was very close to being right. The very next day, the doctors wrote Lina's discharge orders. Since Lina was vomiting about every three hours, I questioned if that was the right thing to do. Lina was actually so weak that she vomited just fifteen minutes before we were scheduled to leave the hospital room. None of that mattered; we were still made to feel like unwanted house-guests that have outlasted their welcome. As the nurse helped me with my frail Lina into the car from the wheel chair, she said with a grin, "Now I don't want to see you two back here!"

I could just imagine some administrator standing at an open window and, with a shaking fist, screaming the exact same thing!

Lina's brother, Casey, and our son, Brian, were at our home when we arrived. Lina was still unable to walk upstairs, so we had to figure out new sleeping arrangements. Without asking, Casey and Brian completely disassembled our large four-poster bed and brought it downstairs. They reassembled it right in the middle of the living room. We put a nightstand next to the bed, and moved the phone to the night-stand, and we were in business! Our bedroom was now downstairs!

We were trying to keep things as normal as possible around the house, but the procession of home health nurses that came by twice a day and the constant phone calls kept our house anything but normal. For the next five days, I did everything the doctors and nurses told me to do, plus I added in lots of Tender Loving Care. Nothing was working, though, and I simply stood by as Lina continued going further downhill every few hours. I had to especially watch her as she slept to make sure that her breathing did not get too shallow or stop completely.

My journal entry from Tuesday, February 11, plainly shows my frustration and anger:

> 8:30 A.M. Regularly scheduled doctor's appointment.
> Lina is *real* sick. When I got her out of the car, she looked

pale and yellow. She continued to vomit heavily in the doctor's office at the cancer center. Doctor tells us that her blood work and lab report aren't good. All levels are low. Recommends re-admission to the hospital. Very weak, heavy vomiting. We get her admitted. Echocardiogram of heart is done again, to keep a close check of the heart valves. More heavy, heavy vomiting and diarrhea. Doctor orders urine and stool samples taken for testing. Mom & Dad, Dina & Bryan are here to pray. Lina and I talk about "plans". We are all crying. It doesn't look good. Please Lord, not now. Give me strength. Give Lina her strength.

For the first time ever, the doctor actually told me that they had done all they could. It was just a matter of waiting to see if she would "turn the corner" all by herself. Given that prognosis, we had to, for the first time, talk about "plans" and verbalize what Lina would like sung at her funeral and how her personal possessions would be split among our two children. That was my first dark day.

Lina was so weak due to malnutrition that we had to start feeding her intravenously. The giant IV bag with the milky liquid seemed to do the job. Within a day, she seemed a bit better. We all seemed comforted to know that she was finally getting the nutrition that she desperately needed.

But, the hospital administration was still leaning hard on the doctors to get us out of the hospital as soon as they could. After just six days, we were sent home again, this time with an IV pole (so we could continue with the intravenous feeding ourselves). Though Lina was feeling better than when she was wheeled back into the hospital, she was still a very sick girl. So ended our third hospital stay.

For the next few days, we ferried back and forth from home to the doctor's offices and back home again. Lina's medical problems just didn't want to get any better. Even more discouraging, Lina's right hip had begun to "click and pop" as she slowly moved in her walker. The orthopedic surgeon got me riled up during one office visit when we were discussing the movement Lina felt in her hip. Incredibly, he matter-of-factly told Lina, "Whatever you are doing when it clicks and pops, just stop doing that."

Lina was instantly depressed, finally worried that her condition might never improve. By now, I was questioning my God, "How could you let this happen?" The clouds seemed to darken as I shook my head in disbelief.

My Worst Day So Far

February 1997

We settled into an uncomfortable routine during the latter part of February 1997. Lina would spend each day unsuccessfully trying to eat something of substance, and would spend the following hours successfully vomiting what she had just tried to digest.

As Lina worsened significantly during this period, there were numerous times I ended my journal entry for the day with, "This has been my worst day so far." Each time I penned that, I truly meant it. Until I actually had to live through it, I could not fathom how the next day could be any worse, short of completely losing her.

In addition to watching Lina get physically decimated, I also had the privilege of watching the two of us get financially abused. We were caught in a firefight between the National Marrow Donor Program and the hospital and our insurance company, with everyone refusing to pay bills (that, of course, had our names on them) until somebody was legally pinned with the blame for the ongoing tragedy.

Though our naval retirement pay was a godsend, it didn't cover much more than our house payment. We usually needed both Lina's and my pay to help make ends meet. Now saddled with medicines, co-payments, and takeout food, we could have used a lot more. In the current situation, Lina was making only one-quarter of her normal wages (the limit of the state's disability coverage) while she was lying on her back, and I wasn't making much more than that while caring for her while she was lying on her back. Thank God we had family, friends, and savings to see us through.

My day-to-day view of medical science was changing, too. I slowly realized that there is much our doctors and nurses know; however, there is equally as much they don't know. When this whole your-wife's-about-to-die affair had started, I had rather meekly stood by and done exactly as the doctors had ordered. As time went on, though, I began inviting myself to the doctor's daily strategy meetings—sitting in the back with my journal, my pen, the latest lab reports, and a medical encyclopedia in my lap—struggling to understand the motives behind and repercussions of each of the doctors' decisions.

Given that increased familiarity, I had, by the end of February, come to appreciate that the doctors were indeed only human, so I would only give their diagnoses credence if and when they could unequivocally convince me that they were 100% sure of themselves. I would not entertain any thought of their discharging Lina until I myself believed it to be in her best interest. I, therefore, spent most of the last part of February deflecting authorizations to discharge.

One last concern: nearly all of Lina's immediate family—her mom, dad, sister, brother, daughter, grandson, and husband—were by her bedside on a daily basis. Brian, our only son, had recently joined the Navy as a shipboard firefighter, and was the only one of the immediate family not privy to our daily travails.

As the unofficial information-provider to all our friends and family, I had the hardest time deciding not so much what to tell our son, but rather what tone to use, when I told him about his mother. If I put too optimistic a slant on the report, Brian would stay at work and hate himself and me forever if his mother unexpectedly died. Too pessimistic a slant, though, and Brian would use up all his leave, spending every day he had at the hospital, watching a situation which could possibly remain stagnant for a very long time. Worse, he might not be given permission to take extended leave, leaving his mind half-focused on his mother and only half-focused on the fires he was supposed to be fighting.

Compared to everything else that was going on, this concern should have been inconsequential; truthfully, my inability to decide how to talk to my own son ate at me nearly every day.

The primary dragons we had to fight in late February were Lina's kidneys. Her renal function had slowed down so much that doctors were forced to continuously transfuse new blood into her system. Almost every day, we would get Lina out of bed, in the car, to the hospital, through the transfusion, and back to bed again.

Once the transfusions had settled her kidneys, Lina reached what is called an unstable equilibrium. The staph did her no more harm, but it took a monumental amount of medication every day just to keep it that way. Unfortunately, the rest of her body–specifically, her large intestine–was not too keen on all the extra chemicals that the medications brought along.

The large intestine is a deceivingly simple device, much like a thin wall, which separates you from what's left of your food. Everything that's still usable as fuel is sucked through the lining of the large intestine into the body; everything that's not usable is left alone to eventually pass outside the body. Unfortunately, the large intestine doesn't quite know what to do with modern medicine's antibiotics. By the time the large intestine gets to play a part in the digestive cycle, any medicines still in the tract ought to be left as waste. Sometimes (especially when there are a lot of different types of antibiotics), they get sucked through the lining, anyway. These inadvertent transfers result in tiny abscesses and small, raw, inflamed ulcers along the lining; the illness the abscesses and ulcers cause is called ulcerative colitis.

All in all, colitis is a rather gross condition. Acute abdominal pain, profuse sweating, nausea, loss of appetite, and diarrhea with blood and pus accompany a 104°F fever. Doctors can relieve some of the symptoms with a drug called sulfasalazine, but the best thing to do is simply reduce the number or potency of the drugs already being taken. That latter approach seemed to be the easiest one to try on my multi-drugged wife, so the doctors stopped one of the antibiotics (Ciprofloxacin), leaving her finally on only one antibiotic (Vancomycin) and on one only-when-absolutely-necessary painkiller (Ativan).

While we waited out the effects of the Cipro withdrawal, Lina's hip began to ache. That complication really depressed Lina. Though I purposely tried to remain upbeat, that complication also nearly broke my spirit. I had truly not seen this as a forever-affair. Deep in the recesses of my mind, I believed that after some short, definitive period of time, Lina would begin to get better and continue getting better until she was finally back to "normal." Instead, Lina's hip had gone from fine (at birth) to sore (after the harvest) to staph infected to full of pus and dead cells to surgically repaired to seemingly fine to clicking and popping to aching acutely and continually. I had never envisioned that the walker could become a permanent part of our lives. Lina had been so active before the harvest that restricting her to a near non-ambulatory state would suck the very life out of her.

One morning, she flung herself back on the bed in disgust and cried, "I don't want to do this anymore; I don't want to be an invalid!" Her anguish instantly reduced me to tears. Her verbalized anger toward the situation reflected my unexpressed frustration at how unfair this whole thing was beginning to seem to me.

All whining aside, though, things were indeed starting to look up. Lina was finally on a single antibiotic and a single painkiller. The staph infection had stopped randomly attacking defenseless body parts. Her kidneys had climbed up from the depths and were slowly making a comeback.

Our lives were once again highlighted by normal adult activities: solid food, semi-solid bowel movements, and somewhat irregular vomiting intervals. I had no choice but to thank God for small, wondrous miracles.

Of course, the fact that we had unwittingly transfused an incurable disease directly into Lina's bloodstream might have tempered my enthusiasm slightly. But, that's the subject for a whole other chapter.

THE PRAYER TRAIL

As Lina began to stabilize, I had some time to take stock of our situation. The one thing that stood out under scrutiny was the incredible number of devoted supporters we had to help us through our ordeal. I wish I had the space to do more than just highlight a small portion of the wonderful support we received. Though I cannot use this chapter to personally thank everyone, suffice it to say that I still read each of the more than 300 get-better-fast cards Lina received, still remember each of the telephone calls which were patched into the hospital room, and still appreciate everyone who at one time or another held my hand, hugged me, and said they were praying for us. The constant influx of support truly kept me sane.

Family

Lina's family was much closer than most I had ever seen. My own mom had done a wonderful job raising my five brothers and sisters and me, but the seven of us would never be what might be termed an "intimate" family. By comparison, Lina's family was some sugary clone of the Cleavers. Mom and dad had married back in 1954 and had only lived in two towns (Artesia and Long Beach) since coming to the U.S. in 1957. Lina, her brother, and her sister had attended all the same schools and had never lived more than ten miles from each other for any extended period of time. Lina's mom watched all the grandkids while her daughters worked.

Nearly every weekend included some type of family get-together for at least one meal.

The outcome of that closeness was predictable. There were family members at Lina's bedside every day. Even our youngest nephew made sure his entire universe was focused on his aunt that he called by his childhood nickname: "Uncle Lina".

> *Dear "Uncle" Lina,*
> *It's Sunday. I hope you get healed. My whole class and school is praying for you and that's including me. I hope you have a good day.*
>
> *Love,*
> *Robert*

Friends

Lina's huge circle of friends adapted to their support role almost immediately. Close friends grew closer, forgotten friends returned to the fold, and mere acquaintances showed their true colors as they developed into wonderful friends.

> *Lina –*
> *You have been so much in my thoughts, my heart and my prayers. You are one of my dearest friends and I am so sorry you have been through so much –*
> *I know God is and will continue taking care of you–I have angels in heaven to remind him.*
>
> *Love –*
> *Cher*

Dear Lina,

It's too bad it took something like your illness to re-cement our friendship, but thankfully it did.

Cher and I have been burning the phone lines worrying and talking about you. And now I hope our prayers have been answered.

We are so happy you are recovering the way you are. You still have some work to do, but it will come. Maybe not overnight, but it will come.

Love,
Wanda

Dear Lina,

I'm so glad to hear you're home. Take good care of yourself, OK? I'm praying for renewed strength, freedom from pain, and rapid progress in being able to walk comfortably. God bless you, my friend.

Hurry and get well. The "Old Broad's Club" needs you to help celebrate.

Love,
Anne

Lina,

*All I can say is, "They better be Damn Sure you are **well** before sending you home this time!"*

We were sure sorry to hear from Papa how terrible last week was for you. We have been praying a lot & you are *always in our thoughts…so make them get you **all** well so we can all go out and celebrate.*

We love you,
Rusty & Carol

P.S. You need another phone line in your room.

Work Relationships

With the velocity of life nowadays, you can never really be certain if your attempts at passing joy and peace to others are successful. The reaction to Lina's absence from the dentist's office was a pretty clear signal of how successful she had been.

Dear Lina,
Just want you to know I have missed you the last few times I have been to the office.

Love and best wishes
Walt

Hi Lina —
Just checking in with you. Wanted you to know I was thinking about you. I still call Sonora to find out how you're doing. I guess you just got out of the hospital again. Gosh, Lina, you've really had "it". I can't wait to see you. When I talked to Sonora the other day, she said you were doing much better. I bet your Boss really misses you. You seem like the type of dental assistant that has everything organized and well

taken care of. If I remember correctly, you've been with him a long time. I bet he can't wait 'till you're back. Besides, it won't be long and you'll be tired of being home.

Let Sonora know when you're up to our visit and we'll be there.

Take care Lina,
Rita

Dear Lina,

I was really concerned when my sister Louise told me about you being so ill. It sounds like you've had a real rough year.

I've been told you have a Great Family. I'm sure everyone is concerned. We're very lucky to have a good family help us through a lot of difficult times. How long has it been since you gave the Bone Marrow Transplant? When Louise told me about the bone marrow transplant, I didn't realize you were so sick, until I called in for an appointment and they said you weren't there.

We want you to know you are in our prayers. Sometimes the load gets really heavy. And I have something I tell my family. God gives you only as much as you can handle.

(He whispered, "My precious child, I love you and will never leave you…when you saw only one set of footprints, it was then that I carried you.") He is always with us. He has carried me through my life several difficult times. You are in our thoughts.

*Love and caring for a **special person** like you is very easy.
You give from the heart.*

Love,
Leroy and Linda

P.S. Here are a few rose petals from our garden.

Church Family

Lina was already attending Emmanuel Reformed Church when we met. Her life circle was intimately tied to Emmanuel: we had been married there, our children were baptized there, and someday my own funeral will be there, too. We had not, however, continued to attend out of some misplaced sense of habit; the Christian family there simply makes us feel as close to Jesus as one possibly can while here on Earth. Without hesitation, all Jesus' soldiers at Emmanuel took up arms to support us through our ordeal.

Dear Lina,
I'm so sorry that you're back in the hospital! I call the "Prayer Connection" at Church regularly to keep up on your condition. You are in my thoughts and prayers and there are many people praying for your healing.
God bless you and your family.

Love,
Kitty

Dear Lina,

You are lifted to the throne of grace many times each day, as we're so deeply concerned for you.

I spent some time alone in the Prayer Chapel praying for you and Gov. The lighted picture of Jesus reaching down to rescue a little lamb encouraged my heart as I visualized His hand reaching down and healing your body. May that thought fill you with **Hope.**

You are loved,
Shirley

All our prayers and thoughts are for you.

I praise God for what He **is** *doing and what He* **will** *continue to do in and through your lives.*

May **all** *Glory and Praises go to Jesus Christ, the author and protector of our lives.*

We love you!
Mitch and Vickie

Dear Governor,

Thank you for the kind words which you left on my tape. Sorry, I was not there to respond. And since our busy goings back and forth in Church do not leave much opportunity for intimate talk, I found it better to also send you this. It is good to hear that the Lord worked through us together with others, certainly more diligent and capable than I. So, any appreciation for me first belongs to the Lord who guides all our circumstances. And then, if any human effort should be recognized, please think of Mieke who was the spiritually stronger (if there is such a thing) of our team. She is gone, but not her influence. It was my privilege to live in the shadow of her noble character, and to be allowed on occasion to work with her.

I thank our Lord for all your diligence in accompanying Lina over her difficult road. And how good is he in providing life and relief. The Lord bless both of you in the midst of your family.

Dirk

Dearest Lina,

God has heard the prayers of His people and He has given you back to us. I could feel the joy around at church on Sunday as we learned the good news that you could come home.

I realize you still have a lot of healing ahead but I pray for you & Governor daily that you will be able to wait patiently as God continues His miracle of healing. The day will come when you are well again!

I'll continue to pray for your daily progress and sometime soon, I hope, I'll stop by for a short visit (when Governor says it's OK).

Besides my love and concern for your life, many others and I have really missed you. You touch so many of our lives in such loving ways.

Love,
Dolores

Organized Support

"For where two or three are gathered in My name, there am I in their midst." In no time at all, individuals who had been praying for us ensured the groups they belonged to were praying just as fervently.

> *Dear Lina,*
> *So very sorry to hear about your illness. We are praying for you, also our Tuesday morning Bible study group in our home is praying for you. You are a special person & God is using you for a purpose.*
>
> *With love,*
> *Harvey & Alice*

> *Oh, how we celebrate this special day with you. We prayed and God answered our prayers.*
> *When you came into Church on Sunday, all of our hearts rejoiced over what God had done!*
> *The women of the Tuesday night Bible study have prayed and will continue to pray for you and your family. Please know you are loved by so many.*
>
> *Sincerely,*
> *Joyce*

> *Dear Governor,*
> *We truly appreciate how supportive you are with the Marrow program. We want you to know we are here for you and Lina. Our department will continue to say our prayers*

for you, Lina, and your family. May God continue to guide you during this difficult time.

> *Sincerely,*
> *American Red Cross*
> *Marrow Donor Program*
> *(with 17 signatures)*

Lina,
You are thought about and prayed for so much. We pray that God will restore you to complete health and bring you back to us very soon.

> *Sheryl & Jerry (in a card with 27*
> *other Adult choir member messages)*

Lina,
We are praying for you at Moms In Touch at Valley Christian. We are praying for God's wonderful supernatural peace to encompass you, that you will be very aware of His presence.

> *Love,*
> *Moms In Touch*

Long-Distance Love

Between our old Navy connections and everyone's current propensity for dialing long-distance numbers, Lina's support group quickly took on nationwide dimensions.

> *My dearest Lina and Gov –*
> *Mom called and said that the hospital told her the good news—you're home! Alleluia!*
> *I pray for you every day. I hope that you continue to improve. I know that those two grandbabies are the biggest incentive, though.*
> *So, Govvy, are you holding up? Has light returned to the world? Lina—I love you. Please don't leave me.*
> *Write and tell me **everything**. Lina, you not only were part of a miracle, you now **are** a miracle!*
> *I know, I know—this is really babbling. I love you both. I miss you. Write me at church: St. Paul Lutheran Church, Yorktown, Texas*
>
> > *God's peace and my love –*
> > *Kay*

> *Dear Lina,*
> *We are so glad to hear you are home from the hospital. Being home has to make you feel much better.*
> *Good ole Nebraska is having a whopper of a snowstorm!*
> *…Hopefully we'll have things looking good by the time you come out next time.*
> *We're really looking forward to seeing all of you. Let us know when we can expect you.*
> *Well, I've got to go out in this nasty weather to walk, so better get going.*
>
> > *See You Soon,*

Judy

Lina —

This has gone on enough now! Man, I was sad to hear you're still having trouble…about now you must feel like "Job Jr." Three months of anything is too much. We just wanted you to know we are praying for quick healing. We love you & have asked our Christian friends here in Colorado to be lifting you up, too.

Talk to you soon, my friend.

Love 'n blessings,
Billie

Strangers

For everyone who believes that life has simply become too unfriendly, uncaring, and impersonal, I present these wonderful "strangers" who heard Lina's story and still found time in their lives to touch our days.

Dear Mr. and Mrs. Joy,

Thank you for shopping at our store for your granddaughter's gift.

It was a pleasure meeting both of you and hearing your incredible story of survival. I will think of it often and be inspired by it.

I look forward to seeing you again soon!

Sincerely,
Eugenie

Lina and family:
I feel like I "know" you, since Marianne shared with me
about how sick you are.
We (hubby & friends) are upholding you in our prayers,
and especially asking God to bless the means that are being
used to help you recover.
We know God will give His Grace to strengthen you and
help you to be patient, and lean on Him.

In His Name,
Ann

Lina,
We have never met but I heard what a wonderful thing
you did for the one who needed the bone marrow. God bless
you!
I'm very sorry to hear of all the problems that came after-
*wards. My precious family prays for you to get well **very soon**.*
(My Jamie who just turned 4 prays for you too! It is so, so
sweet how she loves the Lord and really talks to Him from the
heart!)
I hope we can meet. (I've attended Emmanuel for 3+ years
*and **love it**!)*
Anyway, may the Lord be with you & comfort you through
this tough & painful time. Take care.

Love,
Jennifer

Visionaries

Amazingly, we were even touched by visions provided to modern-day prophets. The peace associated with believing that someone else has actually heard directly from God concerning a loved one is overwhelming.

> *It was sometime in February, when the kidney failure and the skin condition were active. I had fasted and prayed that day for Lina's healing. I believe the Lord gave me a vision both for my own assurance and more importantly Lina's future exhortation. This is what I saw:*
>
> *A very large butterfly had just emerged from its chrysalis (or cocoon). I had never seen a butterfly with such a variety of colors before; and never such **intensity** of color. The butterfly was not flying, but sitting **peacefully** while the sun's light warmed its wings. It was basking in the glory of the warmth of the light. The words accompanying this picture were, "Behold, the old has gone, the new has come."*
>
> *I was so emotionally lifted that day, because I **knew** that Lina would be given her life back. However, the deeper sense I had, which continued to grow as I reflected on the vision over time, was that the physical healing was only the **minor** part of what was happening. The physical healing was merely a vehicle through which the true spiritual healing would occur. The empty chrysalis I saw was limp, fragile and lifeless.*

It no longer had any use—its purpose had been served. I sensed that the Lord had caused the old "outer self" to die, so that a new "inner self" would be available and willing to serve His purposes. I feel the physical peeling of skin was a further physical sign of a deeper work—a vivid "symbol"...

Because of God's miraculous transformation, Lina can "fly." She can see so many more people to whom the Kingdom of God must be brought.

Lina—fly to where your Lord leads you, and there, like the butterfly, reflect the beauty of his glory!

Susan

I believe that only God can move mountains. Lina's family, friends, co-workers, and acquaintances had done what we could to circle that mountain and ask for God's help. If I were God, I would have been pretty impressed with this outpouring of love and healed young Lina right away. The real God, however, seemingly had other plans for our immediate future.

In Sickness

Sunday morning, March 2, 1997

We were waiting for the home health nurse to arrive and start Lina's next dose of Vancomycin. Lina was sitting on the couch in our family room with the IV umbilical attached to her. I was dressed and ready to go to our morning worship just two blocks away.

The nurse was right on time as usual. She would be there, administering to Lina, for about an hour and a half. Perfect for me to get to church and back.

As I was saying my good-byes, the nurse asked me if I had seen the rash on Lina. The rash was a bright red oval spot centered high on her abdomen. As if on cue, Lina started to shake and run a fever. Her extremities were cold, but the rest of her body was warm to the touch. Before our very eyes, the rash spread over her torso in less than an hour. The hospital instructed the nurse to get us to the emergency room as soon as possible! So much for church.

By the end of the day, Lina was in real trouble. The bright red rash had covered nearly all of her body. She was wracked with a high fever and uncontrolled shivers.

The following morning, the infectious disease doctor came into the room, took one look at Lina, and promptly announced, "She has classic Red Man syndrome. We will just change her antibiotic." (The syndrome he was referring to is simply a nasty drug reaction to an antibiotic.) In just forty-eight hours, however, the good doctor would be forced to change his mind.

The bright red color of her skin gave way to a dark purple color that looked like black and blue marks received in a severe beating. Large deep blisters formed on Lina's palms and the soles of her feet. She looked as though she had been in a very serious accident. Then, her body started to swell. At that point, I wanted answers and I wanted them quickly!

Lina was going downhill fast. The doctors told me that it appeared that she might have something viral like measles, or maybe some kind of drug reaction, or maybe something that they had never seen before. We called in a dermatologist to get an opinion. He took a bit of skin from the inside of her left knee for a biopsy. His evaluation: Stevens-Johnson syndrome.

I flew into action as I had learned to do anytime I heard an unfamiliar word, phrase, or drug name. Within a minute, I was deep into my medical encyclopedia reading about this syndrome. Stevens-Johnson is very rare; only 113 cases have been reported in the United States—and only eleven of those survived. Soon after my quick introduction came my questions, fast and furious. How does one get Stevens-Johnson syndrome? What is the course of treatment? How were the eleven survivors treated that resulted in their lives being saved?

The doctors were taken aback at my sudden reaction. I had treated them kindly and with great respect in the past, but their standard reaction time would not be good enough here. As they pondered what do to next, I yelled because I believed my Lina was slipping away.

By nightfall, Lina was having trouble breathing, so we placed her on oxygen. Kathy Leonard and Vickie Vander Wal, two of our friends, stopped by to see Lina. They were shocked at what they saw. Lina did not look like herself whatsoever.

In the morning meeting with the doctors, we discussed treatment options. Her skin seemed to run a predictable course: red rash; followed by raised red welts (each with a very small blister on top); followed by large blisters; followed by smooth, very red, hot, swollen skin that looked like a bad sunburn; and finally, large, dark purple spots that look like deep bruises.

The doctors decided to treat her as though she were a burn victim. They summoned a plastic surgeon to look at her for possible skin grafts. The plastic surgeon—one of the best in the country when it comes to burn victims—was very matter-of-fact. His diagnosis of Lina was actually pretty close to that of the other doctors. He said the problems could have been caused by many things, and that he needed to see the pathology report from the skin biopsy. Again, I yelled, saying that could take days and I wanted a course of action now! The plastic surgeon assured me that, if the deep blisters start to separate her skin layers from her fat and muscle tissue, he would start the skin grafts immediately.

My journal entries, sporadic and now nearly incomprehensible, reflect my increased anger and anxiety during the early days of March:

> Friday, March 7
> At 4:30 A.M., Lina's temperature is 103.6°F. She tells me that she has never felt so bad. Her mouth and throat are full of thrush. Her hands and feet, especially on the palms and bottoms, are purple and swollen with large blood-filled bumps. She has slept most of the day. She has eaten nothing. She is in a lot of pain and she itches from head to toe.

> Saturday, March 8
> Lina could hardly breath by 3:00 A.M. Her stomach has swollen so big that it is pushing on her diaphragm. We had to put her on oxygen. Around 6:30 A.M. or so, Dr. Goldberg *[lead doctor]* came in. About 8:00 A.M., Dr. Kasper *[dermatologist]* came in. Both were encouraged by the reduction in her rash, but both were concerned about

her fluid retention and difficulty in breathing. Dr. Goldberg and I both agree that we should keep her on morphine today to keep her from the near panic she feels about the inability to breathe normally. I went home at 9:00 A.M. to shower and change. By noon, Lina is sedated. Her pulse rate is 120. Her respiration is 60. We are watching her temperature closely and controlling it with Tylenol suppositories. We have increased her fluids to 304 ml/hr (200-saline) (104-TPN). Dr. Goldberg explains that her kidneys are working somewhat. However, we don't seem to be keeping fluid in the vascular system where it needs to be. We are putting all this fluid into her to keep the vascular system hydrated. It seems that the fluids are going into the tissues, instead of through the kidneys and out the bladder. She is not urinating. Any fluid loss is via skin evaporation. Her weight is 185 lbs. She was 159 lbs. just 72 hours ago. It's like a Catch-22 situation, the more fluid we send into her, the more bloated she gets, making it difficult to breathe. We don't want her to use a diuretic drug, because that will only draw more water out of the vascular system adding to dehydration.

By the next morning, I was back into my routine of staying all day and night, leaving at 4:00 A.M. to return by 6:00 A.M. As I stepped back into her room this time, though, I found her bed empty! There was a man in a white lab coat with his back to me staring out the window into the early morning sun. A rush of panic struck me like the blast from an explosion. I stood in the doorway with my feet frozen to the floor. A thousand and one thoughts flew through my mind in the blink of an eye: "She must be gone. How could this have happened during the two short hours while I was away? Why didn't they call or page me? Why did they take her body away so soon? How do I tell her parents and our children?"

The man turned slowly and walked towards me. He had an emotionless poker face. He looked directly into my tear-filled eyes, put his arm around me, and shook my hand with the other. "You must be Mr. Joy. I'm Doctor Brown, the renal specialist. Are you having a bad morning?" The look I gave him must have said it all, because he turned and looked at the empty bed and then back at me. The magnitude of the wrong assumptions I had made finally dawned on him. He face broke into a big smile, and he said, "Your wife is all right. I had them take her downstairs to get an ultrasound done on her kidneys." As I wiped away my tears, I chuckled at my own panic and fear.

Doctor Brown explained that Lina's kidney function did not look good at all. If the ultrasound didn't look good, either, then he said he would have to start her on dialysis. Later that same afternoon, he returned to the room with the decision to do just that.

Vickie, our ever-present friend, and Reverend Korver were both in the room with me. We all watched as a Quintin catheter was installed into Lina's neck directly into the right jugular vein. This large "Y" shaped catheter has the diameter of a man's little finger. Her first series of dialysis using that catheter began that evening. While we sat waiting for her to return to her room, Reverend Korver offered up the only thing we could do: we prayed.

After Lina was wheeled back into her room from dialysis, the visitors started to arrive. Word had spread fast that Lina was not responding to treatment. The outpouring of family and friends had the nurses' station playing traffic cops. At one point that evening, there were about thirty people waiting outside her door to possibly get their last glimpse of their dear friend. Lina was so weak that she was hardly aware of the people in her room.

At 1:00 A.M., Lina's room was finally quiet and dark, except for the blinking lights on the various IV's and monitors hooked up to her. As I sat pondering all the happenings of the last day, I could still hear the echoes of

the well-meant offers to help me. I wrote this down in my journal in the
wee hours of the morning:

> 3/14/97. Everyone is trying to help. They are concerned
> about me. They keep trying to take me out for a cup of
> coffee or a break, some lunch, dinner, something, a place
> to sleep. They all mean well, but don't understand that
> God has prepared me for this very situation. Long
> endurance, isolation filled with stress. I'm okay. It's been a
> while since I was on a submarine mission.

The morning meeting with the doctors was rough. They seemed very
disorganized, throwing all kinds of theories onto the table. Every part of
her diagnosis was looked at from all angles, allowing some new, wild spec-
ulations to be made. Lina's skin biopsies showed some form of auto-
immune disease, but no one could say with any certainty what was
causing it. The prime suspects were:

- A drug reaction to the massive doses of antibiotics
- Stevens-Johnson syndrome from an unknown source
- A lupus-like auto-immune disorder, causing the immune system to
  attack its own body
- (A new one) Transfusion-Associated Graft-Versus-Host Disease

The monster called Transfusion-Associated Graft-versus-Host Disease
(TA-GVHD) may have been the culprit all along. TA-GVHD is a demo-
niacally destructive disease caused by the introduction of "bad" (non-irradiated) blood into the bloodstream.

Transfusions for conditions like Lina's kidney malfunction do not require
the full complement of the blood's capabilities; they do not, for example,
require the transfer of any disease-fighting white blood cells. Since, as discussed earlier in the marrow-matching chapter, it is excruciating to match

leukocytes from non-related donors, and since those leukocytes are not required for simple transfusions, doctors simply irradiate the donated blood to kill off all the leukocytes. That leaves only the red blood cells and platelets in the blood, overcoming the worry that any newly input white blood cells might consider the body's original composition as foreign.

If your immune system is intact when you forget to irradiate some of the donated blood, your own white blood cells can usually quickly kill off the "bad" white blood cells. If, however, your immune system is worn out and tired (from fighting off something like a staph infection) when it gets hit by the bad blood, your few struggling white blood cells have no chance. With a large number of non-irradiated foreign leukocytes roaming free and killing at will in your bloodstream, you are considered to have contracted TA-GVHD. That same TA-GVHD rapidly results in a severe rash, harsh diarrhea, a tremendous fever, acute liver damage, and in most cases, death.

The mortality rate for this disease is over 90%. Even more disconcerting, the less than 10% who do survive do not do so as a result of some medicinal course of action. If you're lucky, you get to live. If you're normal, you die. Medical advances are currently of no consequence here.

Once you've succumbed to TA-GVHD, it actually takes about eight to ten days for it to begin to take a visible effect on your body. Based upon that calculation, Lina probably received her bad dose of blood right after her hip surgery in early February. Ten days later, as we made our way back to the emergency room for the umpteenth time, Lina started going downhill fast.

Initially, the doctors probably mis-diagnosed Lina, and assumed that her symptoms were solely the result of an antibiotic reaction. Do not judge that decision too harshly; the number of reported TA-GVHD cases (less than 130 before 1990) does not make it a very common illness, so the doctors would have had to have been very lucky to have even thought about it. Besides, the odds of surviving TA-GVHD are so poor that incorrect decisions concerning its course usually do not matter. Truth be told, mis-diagnosing Lina actually gave the doctors something (besides twiddling their thumbs) to concentrate on.

The reason for the initial mis-diagnosis was pretty straightforward. Remember that Lina was on a single, very toxic antibiotic called Vancomycin. The side effects of infusing that drug too rapidly into the patient include temporary muscle spasms, skin flushing, itching, and hypertension. If the patient has a really bad reaction to the medicine, the temporary side effects may eventually give way to hearing loss and kidney damage. While the hearing loss may or may not be permanent (depending on the patient), the kidney damage is usually reversible once the patient is taken off the medication.

If you look back over the last couple pages, you can see that Lina started right down that side-effect path. First, she began to shake, shivering almost uncontrollably. Then, she got a rash. Then, the rash started to spread and itch. It was at this point that the doctors stopped the medicine.

Even without the Vancomycin, though, the rash worsened. The spreading rash confused almost everyone. Lina's skin seemed to be burning up very deep inside her, forming blood "bubbles" which pushed outward toward the surface. As stated before, Lina's condition looked a lot like Stevens-Johnson syndrome, an almost-always-fatal medicinal reaction. Unable to combat that problem, the doctors simply held their breath and waited for the last of the Vancomycin to clear her system. Thankfully, the Stevens-Johnson-like effects were very short-lived.

Still without the medicine, however, Lina's kidneys quickly began to fail. This alone finally gave the doctors an inkling that Lina's problems might be more than just a simple adverse medicinal reaction. They could not yet, however, make the leap of faith required to call her situation TA-GVHD, since her liver was not yet in failure. Instead, they assumed that her previous kidney problems had returned with a vengeance, and they spent almost a week trying to battle that foe.

This time, though, her kidneys did not just fail; they found a way to completely eradicate the rest of her vascular system, also. The flow of fluids throughout her body basically ceased. In response, every cell that had fluid tried to hold onto it, no matter how unfiltered or dirty that fluid was. To make the situation even worse, every drop of clean fluid the medical team injected into her body was sucked up by the still thirsty cells and not released.

The fluid retention effects were physically gruesome. Lina, who had walked into the bone marrow harvest at a healthy 148 pounds, and who had dropped to 107 pounds during the worst of her vomiting episodes, was now at 185 pounds and climbing.

The fluid retention also caused Lina's girth to expand. Without an operational kidney, injecting fluids to hydrate her was akin to blowing her up like a balloon. My svelte wife grew bulbous; the rearrangement of her insides made it tortuous for her to breathe. The doctors had to sedate her just to keep her sane.

Then, the monster finally removed his mask. The TA-GVHD took Lina's liver.

Though the doctors had stopped the medicine days before, we all believed that Lina was still simply suffering residual after-effects of the bad dose. The rash and the kidney problems could, without too much fantasizing, be blamed on the Vancomycin. The acute liver failure, however, came out of left field. Too late, the doctors realized they had been tilting at the wrong windmill all along.

At that morning's meeting, the doctors let me know that they were calling in a gastrointestinal specialist for Lina's failing liver. The new doctor was great. He took the time to explain the functions of the liver and what he was looking for. His first act was to do a liver biopsy, and to make some decisions based on the results. A liver biopsy is done with a large needle that is navigated through the right rib cage and into the liver. It is hard to believe that he could actually do that to Lina without any anesthesia. She was barely conscious, anyway. She spent most of the time drifting in and out.

Late that afternoon, Lina's mom and dad–Eve and Case–came into her room. Lina and I love both of them almost as much as we love each other. This time, though, Lina reeled back at the sight of her dad. She looked at me and yelled, "Keep him away from me. I don't know who he is or what he wants." I felt his pain, as his own daughter did not recognize him. Soon after, though, Lina's mind was back to normal; she recognized everyone in the room, and started talking softly to her dad.

Lina then started speaking so softly that we could barely hear her. The three of us gathered in close to hear her faint words. Right then, she stopped talking and looked at us all just inches from her face. She raised her hand slowly and touched each one of our faces with the softest touch anyone could imagine. She slowly gazed deep into each of our eyes. She whispered, "What is wrong? What has happened? Have you guys been in an accident? Have you been burned? It's okay, you'll be okay…"

The moment was truly heaven-sent. The three of us all agreed later that, for a moment, we had been face-to-face with a true angel who was letting us know that everything would be okay. The look on Lina's face was not her own; it was the soft face of one of God's perfect messengers.

Lina's eyes then closed, and she drifted away. Case wept quietly with his face in his hands, and for the first time I realized that, even though I was losing my wife, they were losing their little girl. You could feel the pain hanging heavy in the air like steam in a sauna.

Late that same night, the doctor advised me that we basically had no options. He had to do a liver transplant to save her life. The doctor gave me three locations: Scripps Hospital, Cedar Sinai Hospital, and the UCLA Medial Center.

"Which one is the very best?" was my question.

"UCLA Med, hands down," the doctor quipped.

"Good. What's the schedule?" I shot back.

The doctor told me that if her liver did not stabilize within twenty-four hours, he would send her to the UCLA Medical center via the life flight helicopter.

The rest of the night was quiet, and Lina slept a little too well for me. I was up about every five minutes, checking her breathing. At around midnight, the night nurse came in to talk with me.

She was a tall lady with fine gray hair that she kept short. Her slender frame got lost in the big padded chair she rested in. We talked for hours about each other's lives. I eventually realized that the head nurse had taken this night nurse off the rotation of the ward to be with me and to prepare me. What sweet women these were. The night nurse told me of losing her husband early in her life, never to re-marry. Right then, I believed I made the same decision.

I wondered aloud how many times this incredible nurse had to sit in a room with a husband facing the same plight. We had been very lucky from the very first hospital stay, because they had kept Lina on the oncology ward. The nurses on that ward were a godsend. It takes a very special person to care for the terminally ill, day in and day out. Our night nurse was no exception.

I woke up in my big chair next to Lina's bed. It was 7:30 A.M., and the sun was already up. My nurse companion was collecting her things to go. Her shift was over. She hugged me in a warm, motherly way, and said she would see me when her next shift started that night.

The lab person scheduled to take Lina's blood was late that morning. I watched Lina moan with little reaction to the needle drawing her blood. After that disruption, she fell back to sleep and slept late into the morning. When I tried to talk to her, it was as if she was trying to wake up, but couldn't. She was mumbling something, but she would not open her eyes.

Sitting there by myself, I began to wonder how other husbands had reacted when they were confronted with the thought of losing their wives.

I glanced down at my open church directory in my lap, and saw Clark Vanden Berg's name staring at me. I couldn't believe it! Clark not only had lost his wife to cancer, but also had recently lost his son.

I called Clark around 7:30 A.M. and, by 9:00 A.M., he arrived with our mutual friend, Mitch Vander Wal, in tow. (Mitch and his wife, Vickie, had been there every day. They had been juggling their work and family schedules constantly to find the time to be with us.) Those two large men towered over my six-foot frame and comforted me like their own little brother. Clark is steadfast in his love of the Lord, and was experienced with this walk of the unknown. He was a great sounding board for all my thoughts.

By noon, I was very concerned. I had not seen any doctors the whole day. Doctor Goldberg, our lead doctor, had gone up to San Francisco to meet with a group of doctors from Johns Hopkins to discuss Lina's case, and no one else was apparently willing to pay her any attention.

Her blood oxygen was dropping off fast. The nurses sensed that I was getting anxious and that I wanted some action now. With Doctor Goldberg out of town, someone (namely, me) had to take charge to save my wife.

I continued trying to get her to wake up. I kissed her on the cheek and told her, "I love you sweetheart." She heard me and, without a sound, mouthed back to me, "I love you." After that, she fell perfectly still; no movement whatsoever. I rubbed her face and held her hand. Nothing. I ran to the nurse's station; there, they told me that a neurological doctor was on the way to examine Lina. We cranked up her oxygen to three liters per hour, in a struggle to maintain her blood oxygen above 90%.

When he arrived, the neurologist asked me a battery of questions about Lina. He then performed a series of tests, which included some reaction exercises on the soles of her feet. Without hesitation, he declared Lina comatose.

My world was crushing down on me. It took every bit of energy I had to hold on. I had to hold on for Lina. A second doctor recommended that we get Lina up to the Intensive Care Unit (ICU) to monitor her more closely. All coma patients are kept in ICU as a standard practice, he told me.

While waiting for them to transfer my Lina, I sat alone, quietly staring at her. My thoughts were simple: "Is this how it will all end? Was that little, mime-like 'I love you' my last?"

Lina's mom and dad came in soon after, unaware that their daughter had slipped away into the dark abyss of a coma. Initially, they spoke softly, believing she was just asleep. As I explained the entire situation, Case just sat stone-silent, while Eve simply refused to believe. "She is just asleep. Give her a good shake and she will wake up."

It was heartbreaking to see a mother denying to herself the nightmare that had come upon her family. Finally, Eve broke down and cried. Her sobbing echoed down the halls and carried our grief with it.

Letting Go

5:30 A.M.

I drove our van back to the hospital like I had done too many early mornings before. Was this the day? Glancing at the empty seat beside me, the horrid question leapt into my mind. Would she ever sit in that seat next to me again? Without too much imagination, I could almost hear her laughing at one of my dumb jokes. I could almost see her holding up our little grandson, Rilley. I could almost smell her perfume as we slow danced. I thought, why am I torturing myself? I needed to stay focused on the now. Today. This minute. God, what had I done to deserve this?

As the tears ran down my face, I started to shout at the top of my lungs to my God. "God, are You listening to me? I have prayed and prayed. Everyone has prayed! Why aren't You doing anything? Am I that bad a person? Well, she isn't! She was just trying to help somebody. She was just being a Good Samaritan! If You have to take somebody, take me! Look, God, if You were trying to get my attention, then You did. If this is Your message for me to change my life, then I will!…I'll make You a deal. You save Lina and I will stop…" I began to list all the garbage and wrongs, both big and small, in my life. (I later called this experience my "Let's make a deal" prayer.)

Now, I was brought up in a Christian home, and was well rooted in my faith. However, I never, ever felt that the Lord had spoken to me directly. So, what happened to me next is something that I have a hard time

67

explaining. It wasn't a deep booming voice. In fact, it wasn't really a voice at all. It was more of a feeling or presence, one that was very, very clear!

The Lord basically said to me: I MAKE NO DEALS. HOWEVER, IF YOU HAVE SOMETHING TO CONFESS TO ME, I AM LISTENING.

As you can imagine, I was stunned. I was not scared, and I immediately knew who was speaking to me. I realized just then what the Lord wanted from me; it was the same thing He wants from each of us everyday of our lives. So, I began again with the list of wrongs that I was willing to give up. But this time, there were no conditions attached to my prayer. It was a prayer of confession and forgiveness.

Then, with tears in my eyes, I prayed the hardest prayer I have ever prayed. That early morning, I finally prayed to God, "May Your will be done,"…and I finally, really meant it!

It was at that very moment that I finally gave Lina over to Him. I finally realized that none of the doctors' work, none of my ranting and raving, and none of the million prayers being tossed skyward would save my Lina if *He* did not have it in His plan. Before that moment, I was convinced that I really did not want to know what God's will was. In the dark recesses of my mind, I was selfishly afraid that Lina's work on earth was truly complete. But, after praying for God's will, I finally felt a sense of release. Everything would be okay, just as the angelic voice from Lina's lips had told her parents and me.

When I finally arrived at the hospital, the nurses told me that there was "no room at the inn." (The Intensive Care Unit was full.) Lina had not changed much in the intervening hours. Since we had nothing else to do, we spent the day planning for Lina's trip to the UCLA medical center, scheduled for the next morning. I collected phone numbers and names for people at UCLA. The nurses were all encouraging me with stories of how the transplant of a new liver would improve things. The gastroenterologist told me that, because Lina was considered young and had no previous history of liver disease, she would be at the top of the recipient list. It was just a matter of finding a donor. Isn't that strange, I thought, now we are looking for a donor to save Lina's life.

Late afternoon, and still no bed in ICU. Lina's breathing had become very shallow. Case and Eve, Dina and her husband Bryan, and Lina's sister Marianne were there. One of the doctors had told us to keep talking to her, even though she was not responding at all. Medical science doesn't know if a comatose patient can hear you or not.

I was standing in the doorway of her room, looking down the hall for the nurse. The rest of the family was gathered around the bed. Dina lifted her mom's left hand and placed it onto her baby-swollen belly. "Can you feel the baby kicking, Mom? This little girl is active!"

"Hey Dad! She's responding!" Everyone was excited. I hadn't seen anything. I had my back turned.

"What did she do?" I asked.

"She started to get excited and was breathing real fast."Just then, Lina started doing it again. Her chest heaved rapidly as she grasped for air in short quick burst. I really didn't know what to think of it. I didn't know if she was coming out of the coma, or if she wasn't getting enough oxygen, or something worse. Strangely, everyone looked at me as though I was the medical expert, capable of rendering some quick explanation as to what was happening.

I calmly stepped out of the room and called the head nurse over to take a look. The two of us walked back together into the room, and saw Lina still going through the same gyrations. The nurse stopped dead in her tracks, spun on one foot, and ran to the door yelling, "She's Cheyne-Stokeing!! She's Cheyne-Stokeing!!" A throng of nurses rushed the room and started shouting orders.

"Clear the room!–Unplug the bed!–Call ICU and let them know we are on the way…STAT!–Bag her!–Governor, grab that IV pole and follow close to her bed!–Get out of the way!–Here we go!"

It was like any emergency scene on television. Ready or not, we were on our way to ICU! Two nurses ran down the hall, pushing Lina's bed to the elevator; I was close in tow, trying to keep up with the IV pole. Lina's big bed just fit into the elevator. I was pressed hard against the back wall. Another nurse was at Lina's side with an ambulatory bag forcing air into her with every pump. The last nurse had to jump onto the foot of the bed in order for the elevator doors to close.

On the fourth floor, the ICU staff was waiting to assist the instant the doors slid open. Someone took over my position as IV assistant. In less than a minute, the maddening rush was through the double doors of ICU, and all was quiet.

Eventually, I caught up and started through the double doors, only to be stopped before I could enter. "Sir, please let us do our job," the nurse said with a hand raised like a traffic cop.

"But, but that's my wife!" I pleaded.

"I know, so just let us work on her, and someone will be out in a moment to brief you."

I was left standing in the hall, staring at the floor, all alone and helpless. When I heard the elevator door ring, I raised my head. The rest of the family had finally caught up to me.

We all stood looking at each other in disbelief. We found our way to the ICU waiting room. Not surprisingly, there were other families sitting in the quiet room with the same I-can't-believe-this-is-happening-to-us look.

What seemed like hours was really just forty minutes. Finally, two doctors came to the ICU waiting room and asked for me and me only. I stepped into the hall and listened as they, in a matter-of-fact tone, explained the meaning of the seemingly magic phrase that had whipped the nurses into action. Cheyne-Stokes is a syndrome of short shallow breathing, followed by heavy gasping of air. It usually happens just prior to complete respiratory arrest. That was exactly what occurred in our case: Lina went into respiratory arrest just as she was wheeled into ICU.

The doctors told me she had stabilized and was now breathing on a ventilator. "So, how does it look?" I asked, looking the two of them straight in the eyes. I looked to them for the truth and no sugar coating. I also looked, however, for some tell-tale sign of body language to let me know if those two were coming clean with me. I didn't have to look too hard. One doctor had tears well up in his eyes, so he turned and walked away without a word. "What do you say?" I asked the other. "You've been a straight shooter so far. Tell me the truth."

"Doesn't look too good Gov," he said.

"Not good over the long-term, or not good tonight?" I asked.

"I'm sorry Governor, but I don't think she is going to make it tonight."

I looked at my watch; it was 11:20 P.M. "Tonight" had only a few more hours left.

I told the rest of the family about everything except the last conversation; they had already had enough anxiety for one night.

The ICU staff was much stricter than the oncology staff, and they would not let me spend the night in the hospital. I asked to see Lina for just a moment and was denied. They were still working on her.

I got home about midnight. Couldn't sleep, though; I kept thinking I heard the phone ring.

At 6:00 A.M., I introduced myself to the night staff in ICU and asked again to see Lina. Finally, they led me into her room; it looked like a big square aquarium full of beeping monitors, lights, hoses, and IV's. As I walked around, I could barely make out my Lina lying deep in the bed. The large, double hoses from the ventilator were slowly forcing each mechanical breath into her.

The room was very Spartan compared to the one in the oncology ward. No warmth, no flowers. Just functional. Surprisingly, Lina was packed in ice bags. The ICU nurse told me that not only did she arrive in full respiratory arrest, but she also ran an extremely high temperature of 106°F. "That is one tough girl you have there."

SANTO

When I started this story, there was one other major person involved: Santo. This chapter describes the last days of his life.

Lina's marrow was Santo's third attempt at staving off death. His first bout of leukemia had been kicked into remission with a bone marrow transplant in 1989. The leukemia came back again in 1994, but was quickly beat back down with a second transplant. So, when Santo's white blood cell count dropped a third time in late 1996, doctors knew they needed to act quickly.

Santo and Diane never truly expected a donor match. They had exhausted most of Australia's resources to pull off the second transplant. So, instead of approaching their situation with unbridled optimism, they chose to face it with a sense of measured realism. The children, old enough now to understand, had been told what to realistically expect. Santo's will had been updated, and his good-byes had all been started.

The arrival of Lina's name and blood sample was a godsend. A six-of-six match from an unrelated donor on another continent was a fantastic answer to their prayers. Quickly, Santo and Diane began focusing on possibilities.

And just as quickly, Santo and Diane began reeling from the transfusion. Unlike the previous two transplants, Santo was decimated this time by a high fever and staph infection within one day of marrow receipt. Half a world away, Lina was wheeled into an emergency room suffering identical symptoms.

An aggressive course of medicine kept them both around for Christmas. For a family that had said their good-byes in October, Santo's kids relished in the joy of a pleasantly unexpected Christmas with their dad.

By New Year's Eve, though, the multiplicity of the staph infection and his still-depressed immune system drove Santo back to the hospital. By coincidence, Lina's Picc line clogged on New Year's Day, driving her back to the hospital at nearly the very same time as her marrow-mate.

Both the donor and the recipient spent the next six weeks fighting stomach and intestinal problems. Lina escaped the hospital on the 6th of February; Santo escaped on Valentine's Day. In retrospect, Lina had probably left too early, which forced her to spend her first days at home struggling to improve. Conversely, Santo left the hospital somewhat healthy, and got to spend the next week buying gifts and making the most of his homecoming.

But, the joy was not to last. Nearly simultaneously, both of them returned to the hospital with rashes which would destroy their skin. Both of them would begin to have vision problems: Lina began to see things; Santo went blind. Both of them slipped into a coma.

And, on the 14th of March, 1997, Santo slipped away from the bonds of this earth. Finally, he was without pain, without fear, and with the Lord.

POSTURING

Doctor Goldberg returned from San Francisco and went straight to Lina. When we finally met, he told me that Lina was a very sick lady. (I thought to myself, "NO KIDDING!") He also told me that they had detected a "gram negative" bacterial infection in Lina's blood stream, which could have been the cause of the coma and respiratory arrest. He also said there was an antibiotic which could eradicate the infection. That gave me some hope, but I had been down the path of high hopes too many times before to completely believe him.

Because of Lina's comatose condition, the neurologist wanted to run another CT scan on her to take a look at her brain. Her electroencephalogram (EEG) had showed classic comatose brain waves, but he wanted to use the scan to look for damage. Unfortunately, the CT scan had to be done by first removing her from the safety of her ICU room.

Case, Marianne, and I remained in the ICU waiting room while Lina had the CT scan done. Hours went by, delaying what should have been a simple forty-minute procedure. I paced the hallways like an expectant father. Three hours and nothing! I kept calling into the ICU ward, until they got upset and asked me to please stop disrupting them. Finally, though, a nurse peeked into the waiting room and motioned for me to come out. All three of us rose, but she said, "Only Governor for now, please."

I stepped into the hallway, and followed her as she led a fast-paced walk down towards Lina's ICU room. Throughout the short walk, she said nothing and didn't look back. About halfway down the hall, she stopped unexpectedly and turned into the doctors' lounge. I assumed that she just had to get something before going into the ward, but she held the door open and asked me to step in. The room was full of doctors, nurses, the social worker, and the chaplain. I was taken completely off-guard at the sight of this group, and the panic of death gripped me again.

Every eye was upon me, but no one was saying a word. "She's gone. Isn't she?" I said and asked, with all the courage I could muster.

"No," one doctor said quietly. "But your wife had a very serious and massive seizure during her CT scan. She was bleeding pretty heavily from her nose and mouth. We got the bleeding to stop by cauterizing some blood vessels. She is stable again for now, but we do not believe that she can survive another episode like that. Her body is very weak."

After that short burst of information, they sent me back to the ICU waiting room. Again, I had to be the bearer of the grim news to the rest of the family. Case and Marianne just couldn't believe it. "How long do we walk through the valley of the shadow of death?" they pleaded. "Is this the best it will ever get?"

I tried yet again to find a middle-of-the-road attitude to calm my frayed nerves. I continually got over-jubilant with every tiny morsel of good news and then, just as often, got thrown into the dark depths of despair. For my own sanity, I had begun to try to stay focused only on what needed to be done for that very moment, and to not let the dark fear of tomorrow cloud my mind. I was not overly successful in that endeavor.

Finally, we got to go into Lina's ICU room to look at her. The only clue we had that something bad had happened to her was the presence of some residual dried blood in her hair that the nurse was cleaning away. Lina was still buried in a mass of tubes, wires and hoses. Her eyes were gently closed, and her body was still completely motionless, except for the mechanical breathing of the ventilator.

As I sat there late into the night, Doctor Goldberg came to visit with me. I asked him about the liver transplant and if we were still going to do it. He just slowly shook his head. "We are just fighting to keep this girl alive at this point," he told me sorrowfully.

I knew right then that this man was fighting to save my wife harder than he had ever fought for any other patient he had ever had. He shared the same lament I had heard over and over again: THIS IS JUST NOT FAIR!

I told him the fairness issue finally didn't matter to me. It really didn't matter what had brought Lina to this point. It didn't matter if it was a couple of units of un-radiated blood that caused the TA-GVHD, or some auto-immune response to the infection, or a huge reaction to all the antibiotics. It just didn't matter at this point. Doctor Goldberg finally, reluctantly agreed.

In our quiet time together, we talked of our faith. He told me that, although our faiths differed on a belief in Jesus Christ, we believed in the same God. We laid our religions aside and, as two men in a somber place, we prayed to God for Lina. I knew God heard our prayers; I just wondered how He would answer them.

The next days brought no changes. No responses whatsoever. The neurologist came to brief me on Lina's status. Again, I was amazed at what we did not know about the complex human machine that God had put together. We didn't know if Lina would ever recover from this coma. We didn't know if Lina would be comatose for years to come, or if she would die suddenly. There had been all kinds of cases, with all kinds of final outcomes. So, I again tried to prepare myself for any and all possibilities.

I was really shocked when my old friend Alan Meerscheidt–who had served with me aboard my very first submarine–and his wife Megan walked into the hospital. They had jumped on a plane and flown in from San Antonio just to see Lina. Every bit of help was a shot in my arm, including their prayers and support.

The very next day, though I had promised myself I wouldn't, I became ecstatic one more time! In the middle of the afternoon, Lina moved! She did it all by herself. At first, I thought that I was imagining it. Then, after a few minutes, she moved again. She was moving her whole arm. I called the ICU nurse right away. She was as happy as I was, and went to page the neurologist. I then noticed that it wasn't one arm, but both! Her movements increased with regularity to one about every three or four minutes. Within a half-hour, the neurologist arrived, and I ran into him out in the hallway. We were all smiles. With a big grin, he asked, "What's all this talk about Lina starting to stir?"

As we slowly walked towards the ICU double doors, the doctor asked me to explain in detail just what Lina was doing. "Well, she moves both arms at the same time. She is not moving her hands or bending her elbows. She lifts her shoulders in a 'hunching' motion. It's like she is trying to wake up, or maybe she is aware of all the IV lines or something. Whatever it is, it's good!"

The smile ran from the neurologist's face. His pace slowed. I tried to read him, but wasn't sure what to think. Why the somber face at this time of great hope?

The doctor was very methodical in his examination of Lina. Then, he turned to me with "the look" that I had seen way too many times before. He asked me to sit down.

"What Lina is doing is called 'posturing'. I've seen this many times before. This is a reflex-type response that the body goes through when there is severe brain damage and the body and brain are shutting down. She has but a few hours left. It is time to call the family and clergy."

I was so ecstatic, only to have my emotions crushed one last time before we had the chance to do anything. Though I had said it almost flippantly too many times before—that a certain day had been "my worst day so far"–I finally came to appreciate right then and there the sheer magnitude of the horror which a single dirty needle could inflict.

As I cried over my comatose wife for the last time, I was at least thankful that she could not consciously feel the pain or sense the fear associated with all that her body was going through. I prayed for the repose of her soul, brushed the hair away from her now-peaceful face, and quietly departed the ward.

DON T LEAVE US

Dear Mom,

Right now I am so scared! I don't want to lose you! I don't know if you realize it but you are one of my best friends and I love you so very much. I am not ready for my children to grow up without their Oma. You are such a wonderful woman and I can't let people not know you! I am at a point where I don't know what to say or think anymore; you are so giving and loving. I just can't bear the thought of having to go on without you! I pray all day for you! I don't know how God is working on you, but I know He is. I know you can hear me when I talk to you but you can't respond, so I'm writing this letter to tell you later when you wake up. I will continue to talk to you, though, because I know you can hear me. I just want you to know that there are so many people praying for you that the angels must be going crazy up there with all the work they have to do to fill people's hearts to know you're okay, and God must be so busy listening to all the prayers that it's like not being able to answer 100 phones ringing all at once constantly. Well, I love you and I'll write again tomorrow.

I love you.

Dina

EASTER

Lina continued to "posture" until about 3:00 A.M. the following morning. Then, for no apparent reason, her hunching began to slow down. Soon after, she quit hunching completely. The posturing now complete, I figured it was finally time for my Lina to die.

By 8:00 A.M., though, nothing had changed. When the neurologist reappeared during morning rounds, he simply could not figure out what was keeping her alive. He speculated that Lina's brain tissue was possibly shrinking away from her cranial wall, so he ordered an MRI of her skull. I gave my consent without an argument; it's pretty hard to care about more tests when your wife has finished making all her preparations to die.

I really needed someone to talk to, so God had the staff from the National Marrow Donor Program introduce me to Anissa Ayala–an incredible young lady and another testament to God's boundless blessings–who was visiting the hospital that morning. Since the MRI, like all the other major tests Lina had undergone, could not be done in the hospital, but had to be done in the medical center across the street, Anissa and I went down to the first floor's rear lobby to watch them load my catatonic wife into the ambulance for transport, and then just stayed there talking.

Lina's trip over to the medical center looked organized and quiet, but forty-five minutes later, her trip back was a completely different story! The team rushed to get her into the hospital. The one glimpse I had of my wife was simply horrific: her head was lying over to the right side, and her eyes were wide open in a fixed stare. She must have suffered another seizure and died.

I looked at Anissa, but I didn't initially say a thing. Finally, I took a deep breath and unconvincingly whispered, "I must not get upset, I must maintain a middle-of-the-road attitude." Then, I ran like a madman for the ICU waiting room.

Once there, Anissa and I sat together in silence. No one called for us or paged us. After ten eternally-long minutes, I whined, "I can't stand it anymore. Let's go check on her!"

As the two of us arrived at the now infamous double doors to the ICU, the nurse stepped out and, with a big smile across her face, said, "Mr. Joy, I have a surprise for you."

When I walked into Lina's room, my wife–miraculously no longer comatose, catatonic, or near death–followed my progress around the room with her eyes. I was instantly reduced to tears.

I kissed Lina on one of the few bare spots on her forehead, A single tear rolled down her cheek.

When the neurologist arrived soon after, he too cried tears of joy. That was the only time in his career he had seen anyone so close to death regain consciousness.

That first day, Lina was much too weak to move anything, so we taught her to use her eyelids to blink once for yes and twice for no. Within twenty-four hours of her startling recovery, though, she had improved so much that she was taken off the ventilator and allowed to breathe on her own. When the large plastic airway was removed from her throat, she took her first few breaths like a newborn baby filling its lungs on its own power for the first time. As our son, Brian, and I stood by, Brian joked, "I'll bet you're glad to have that thing out of you!"

In a raw, raspy voice, she said, "Yes," and then motioned with her head for the two of us to come closer. With our ears close by so she wouldn't have to strain her voice, she said, "Can I have a Diet Coke®?" Right there, I knew she was feeling better! Everyone close to Lina knows that her worst vice is her near-addiction to Diet Coke®. Those few little words—truly the most wonderful words I have ever heard—finally let all of us know that Lina was back among the living!

Even though she made consistent physical improvement, it took some time for her to regain all her mental faculties. She still has no waking memory of the first few days after coming out of the coma. She would look around and not know where she was or how she got there. It didn't seem as if she was frightened at first, but you could tell it was hard for her to formulate any coherent thoughts.

Each time she woke up, it felt like she was starting over. We had placed a picture of her and me—taken during a cruise two years earlier—on the wall facing her bed. At first, she didn't even know who the people in the picture were. Then, the faces became familiar, but she couldn't think of their names.

Words and sentences did not come easy at first. You could tell it was frustrating for her not to be able to communicate her needs and feelings to those around her. I was there with her almost all the time, but if she woke up and I wasn't there, she became very frightened about being alone.

Our kids and family would all come to see her and reassure her that she was going to be fine. Amazingly, she couldn't understand why they kept saying that. One day blurred into the next. It took her a while to figure out whether it was night or day, and to remember what day it was.

On one occasion, she even thought that she had missed the birth of our second grandchild, Paige. Her days were so confusing that she thought she had been in the coma a lot longer than she actually had been. Thankfully, God had sent her back before she had missed little Paige's arrival.

Eventually, she even succumbed to a fear called, "Sundowners Syndrome," which scared her into believing that if she went to sleep, she wouldn't be able to wake up again. Even with me sleeping on the cot next to her, she would lie awake until the sun started coming up again. As soon as it was daylight, she would close her eyes. Sometimes, she even got angry when I would fall asleep easily, and she would be forced to just lay there and listen to me snore.

Most of all, though, she felt an overwhelming urge to keep telling all those around her that she loved them. She would cry when she thought that she almost slipped away without telling all the wonderful people in her life that she loved them.

In total, Lina spent five days in the coma. During that time, she worsened significantly day by day. On the sixth day, without given any premonition that this day would be different than all the others, Lina awoke.

Miraculously, the Lina who returned from the depths did so very nearly intact: improving liver and kidneys, no internal infections, no desire to vomit, and no diarrhea. How had she recovered? For those of you who have maintained an interest in the medical explanations throughout this story, you will be somewhat disappointed with my answers here, because no one has the slightest idea how she did it.

Numerous questions remain to this day: Had Lina's coma actually been a self-repairing mechanism, an attempt by her mind to outwit her illnesses? Had any of the medicines or procedures assisted in her improvement? Were the staph and the TA-GVHD completely eradicated? What assurances were there that those diseases and their associated side effects would never return? Unfortunately, I do not have the answers to these questions. Honestly, my joy at having Lina back precludes me from caring if I ever do.

Lina had never been so excited about life. Soon after she had come out of the coma, the kids and I arranged to sneak her from her room to remind her what the sun felt like. Her words about that foray show just how thankful, joyful, and peaceful she had become:

> On Easter Sunday, I had been out of the coma for about a
> week. It had been a month since I had been outside. The

last time I was outside, it had been rainy and cold. That morning, as I looked out my hospital room window, I saw a beautiful bright day. Gov and the nurses had conspired to let me see the rose garden on the hospital grounds. They put me in a giant wheelchair, wrapped me in blankets, and put a mask to cover my face. (Boy, I must have looked cute!) The nurses held the doors to the elevator open while Gov wheeled me out. As we came out of the hospital, I felt the warmth of the sun. Governor wheeled me into the garden. It was awesome to see the works of God's hands. The colors of the roses were so bright that they actually hurt my eyes. There were giant puffy white clouds all over the sky. As a gentle breeze blew across my face, I told Gov, "I think God just kissed my cheek." I knew in that instant that my life had been restored. I felt the power of the Resurrection. From that day on, I knew that God still had plans for me. I didn't know what those plans would involve, but I knew that only by God's mighty hand had I been rescued and would I forevermore be led.

TESTIMONIAL

Lina Joy's Testimonial Message
Emmanuel Reformed Church
April 27, 1997

"I want to give glory to God. Thank God for this life renewed.

This has been such an incredible journey. Thank you, Lord, for the miracle of life You've given me—for unchanging, steadfast love, and mercy, and grace. Grace stacked on grace. Praise Jesus for Your gift of eternity, and for the Holy Spirit that fills this place.

I'm so overwhelmed by the power and the love and the support of the family, the friends, this body of Christ, the people that I've never met—people from around the world that prayed and prayed and prayed. I thank you for your prayers. I thank you for the Prayer Warriors that just prayed. Prayer works! I wouldn't be here without it!

The prayers of healing are just so awesome! Learn to build your treasures on God, family, friends, not on the things of this earth, because it can all disappear in a heartbeat. I'm celebrating a life. This is what it's all about: praising and giving God the glory.

You don't know how wonderful it is to hear music, to see sunshine and color, and to sing one of my favorite hymns, 'Trust and Obey.' Trust and obey.

I praise God for my husband. Anyone can be a promise maker; it takes someone special to be a promise keeper. And, this man is a promise keeper. He never left my side.

Thank You seems like such a small phrase in comparison to what all of you have done. You don't know how the cards, the calls, the flowers, the food, the concern, and most of all, the prayers of healing helped me get through each trial. Thank you, people of God. Thank you, Emmanuel. Thank you, friends.

Another thing I praise God for is for the bone marrow program. People, this is a really vital, vital thing. And, they work to save lives. And, I would ask you: don't be discouraged, and don't be afraid. This was a once in a million thing that happened to me. And, there are people out there waiting–they need your prayers, but they need your blood. And, if I had to do this over again, I would. I would, because there's somebody out there that needs a little piece of me to be a part of God's miracle. And, we are all miracles. Every day that God lets the sun shine down on our faces when we wake up, we are miracles. And, we are to be about going out there and sharing the miracle of life that we have here. Sharing that with every single person that we meet–because that's what we're called to do. We're called to be Disciples of Christ, and we're called to glorify God. Give Him all the glory and all the praise; He is so awesome!

And, that is one thing that I've learned through all this: I've learned that nothing is more precious than eternity in Christ, and sharing that with somebody else.

Although my recipient only lived three months, he had three more months with his family than he would have had if I hadn't given. And, praise be to God, he might have found God–found life eternal–in those three months. I don't know.

All I know is that I'm called, I've got a purpose, and so do you. He's got a plan for each and every one of us. You don't know what that is; we're just called to give up our will, and surrender to His will. And, that's what it's all about.

So, people of God, body of Christ, Emmanuel Reformed Church: keep on praying!"

Afterword

Don't get me wrong: just because Lina woke up again doesn't mean that everything is rosy. More than two years after the harvest, Lina's rash still refuses to completely disappear, her hip feels about twenty years older than the rest of her body, and she has never recovered the month of memories lost to the coma. But, she is alive. Which makes me smile.

When I started this book, I stated that I hoped to help teach you what you might do if you found yourself in a situation similar to ours. Though there is much advice I could conceivably pass on, let me leave you with just these three thoughts:

- Always humbly appreciate the yeoman efforts of the doctors and nurses assigned to assist you.
- Always treasure each moment spent with your wife or family; search hard for ways to have more of those moments.
- Always remember that you have no idea what God has in store for you during any of your tomorrows, so make the most you can out of each of your todays.

To all those who prayed for us, again I say thank you. Thank you for helping make all my wishes come true.

Governor C. Joy
December 1998

ABOUT THE AUTHORS

Governor Joy was born in Los Angeles, California. He retired from the United States Navy after riding six different submarines in a twenty-year span. He still resides in the Southern California area with his wife and two adult children. This is his first book.

Bobby Alvarez was born in Caguas, Puerto Rico. He spent six years in the United States Air Force flying F-16 fighter aircraft. He recently earned a Ph.D. in engineering. Bobby is happily married and has two wonderful children. This is his second book.

REFERENCES

The American Medical Association Family Medical Guide. Jeffrey R.M. Kunz and Asher J. Finkel, ed. Random House, New York, NY. 1987.

"Beyond the Call." Denise Grady. Time Special Issue, *Heroes of Medicine*. Volume 150, Number 19, Fall 1997, pp. 69-70.

"BMDW Annual Report 1995." Bone Marrow Donor Worldwide Registry Web page. http://bmdw.leidenuniv.nl/annrep.

Complete Drug Reference: United States Pharmacopoeia. Consumer Reports Books, Yonkers, NY. 1996.

"Demographics of a Blood Donor." American Red Cross Web page. http://biomed.redcross.org/home.

Ellie, A Child's Fight Against Leukemia. Jonathan B. Tucker. Holt, Rinehart, and Winston, New York, NY. 1982.

Fighting Infection: Conquests of the Twentieth Century. Harry F. Dowling. Harvard University Press, Cambridge, MA. 1977.

Fundamentals of Anatomy and Physiology, Third Edition. Frederic H. Martini. Prentice Hall, Englewood Cliffs, NJ. 1995.

HLA and Disease Associations. Jawahar L. Tiwari and Paul I. Terasaki. Springer-Verlag, New York, NY. 1985.

"Introduction to HLA Genetics." L.U. Lamm and L. Degos. *Histocompatibility Techniques*. Heather M. Dick and F. Kissmeyer-Nielsen, ed. Elsevier/North Holland Biomedical Press, Amsterdam, Holland. 1979.

"The Major Histocompatibility Complex Genes and Their Transcriptional Regulation." Sarki A. Abdulkadir, et al. *MHC Molecules: Expression, Assembly, and Function.* Robert G. Urban and Roman M. Chicz, ed. Chapman & Hall, New York, NY. 1996.

"NMDP Online-Patient Information – Feb 10, 1998." National Marrow Donor Program Web page. http://www.marrow.org/cgi-bin/php.cgi.

"Page for the General Reader." American Society of Histocompatibility and Immunogenetics Web page.
http://www.swmed.edu/home_pages/ASHI.

The People's Cancer Guide Book. Ronald E. Aigotti. Belletrist Publishing, South Bend, IN. 1995.

"Share Life." National Marrow Donor Program brochure. National Marrow Donor Program, Minneapolis, MN. 1997.

"Transfusion-Associated Graft-versus-Host Disease." Kenneth Anderson. *Journal of Clinical Oncology.* Volume 9, Number 10, October 1991, pp. 1727-1730.

"Vancomycin." http://www.dadechemistry.com/clinicalhtm.